TEST COLOR PAGE

Thank you for choose this coloring book.
I hope you will have fun.

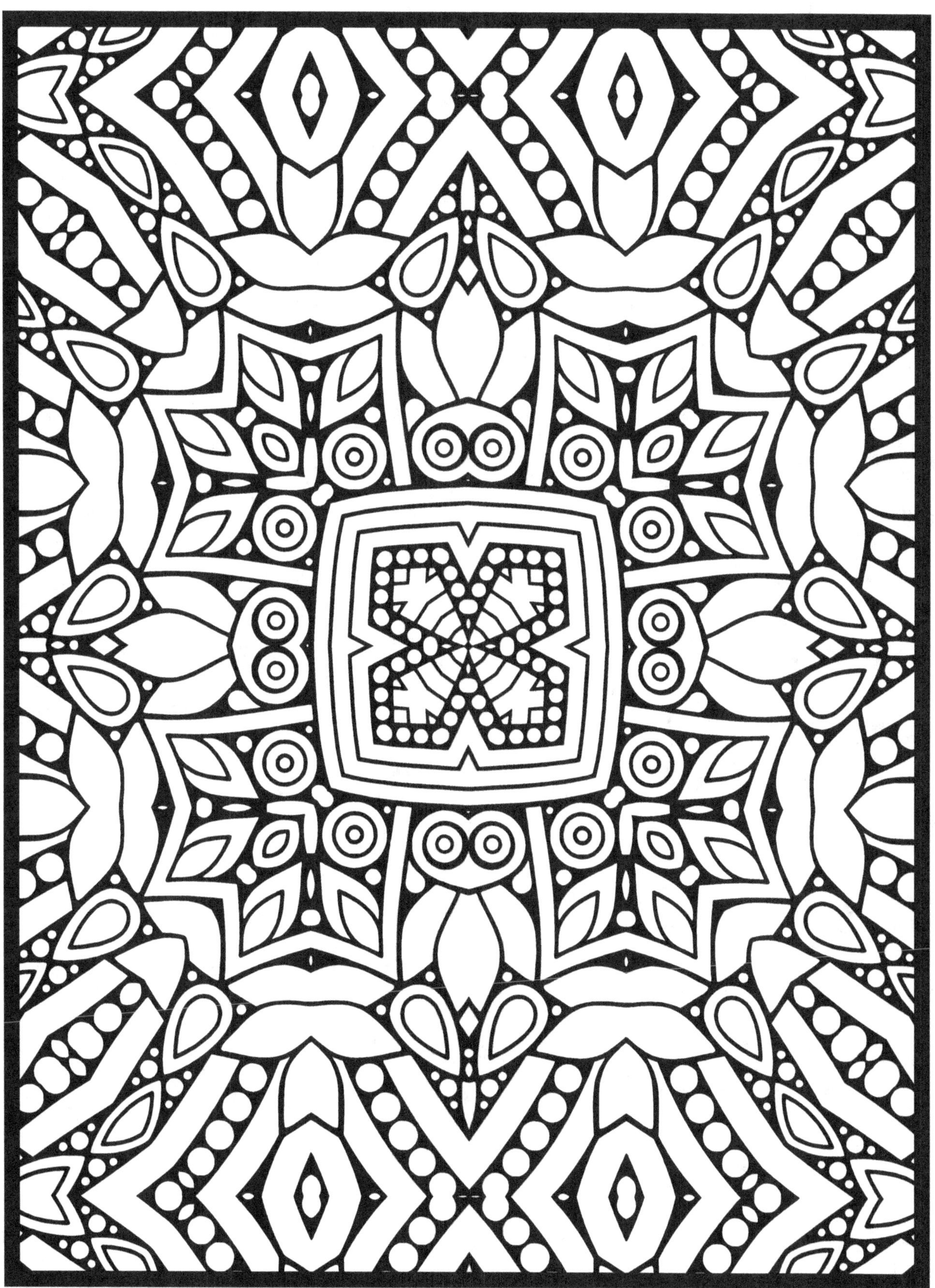

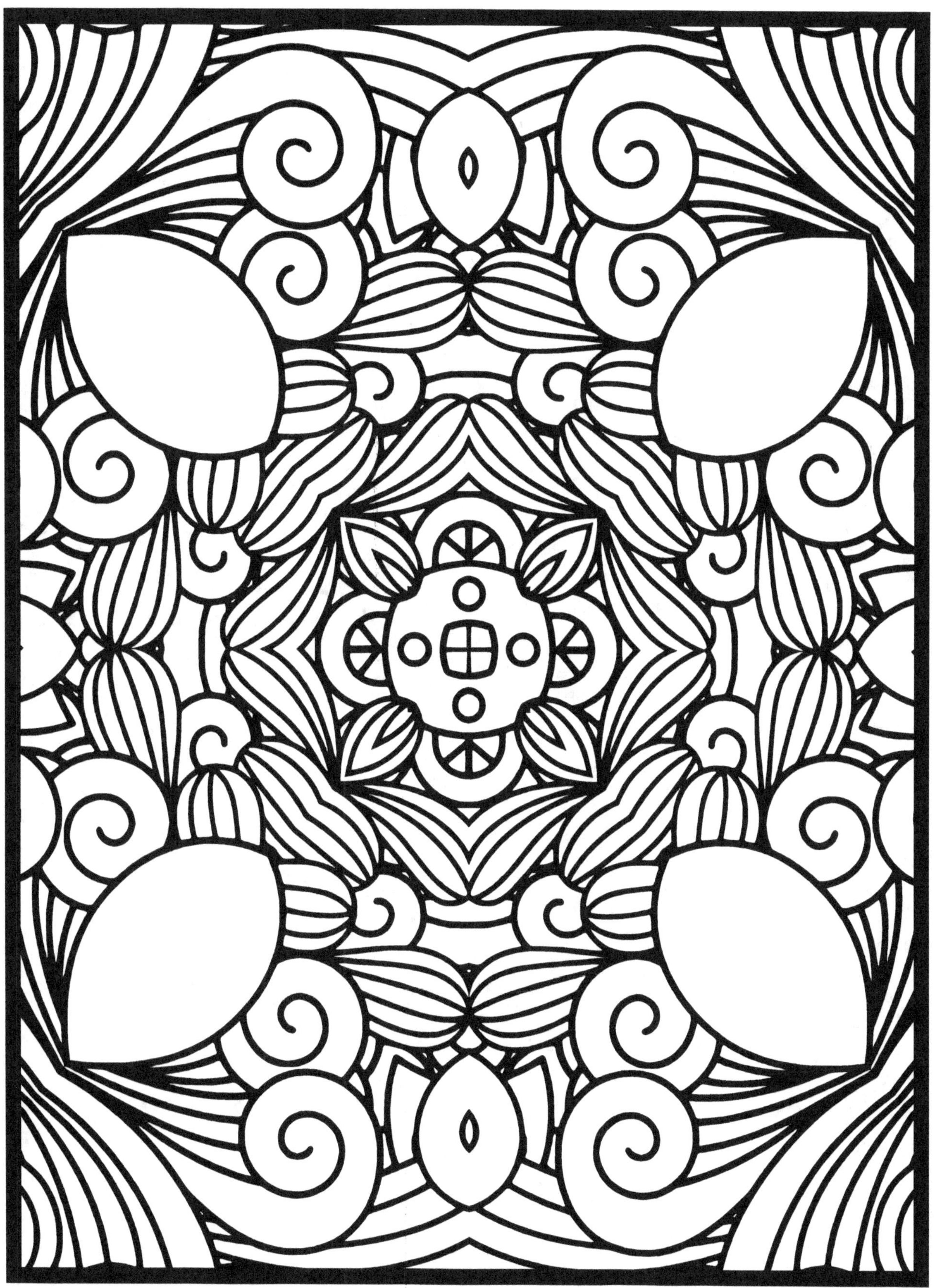

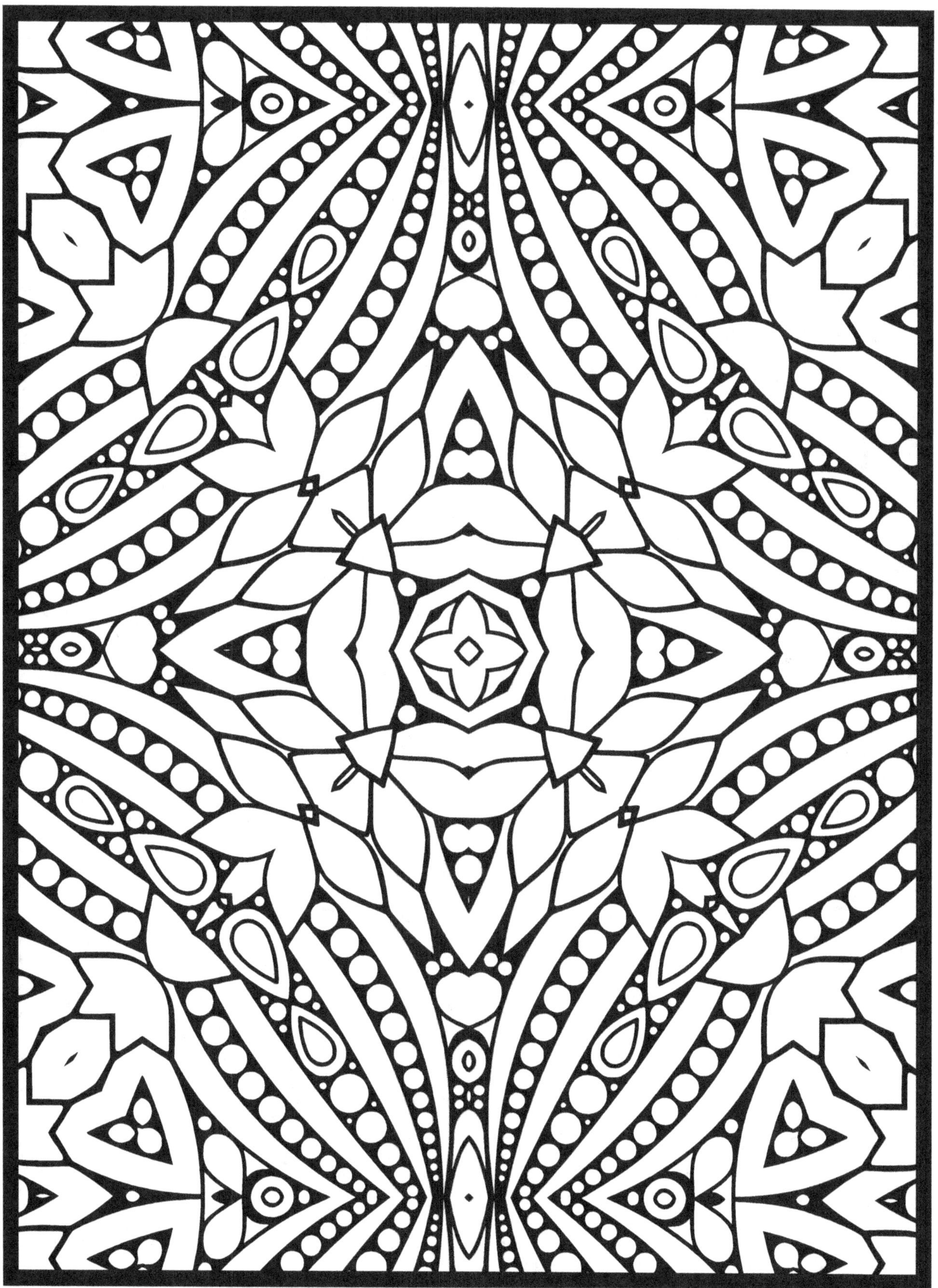

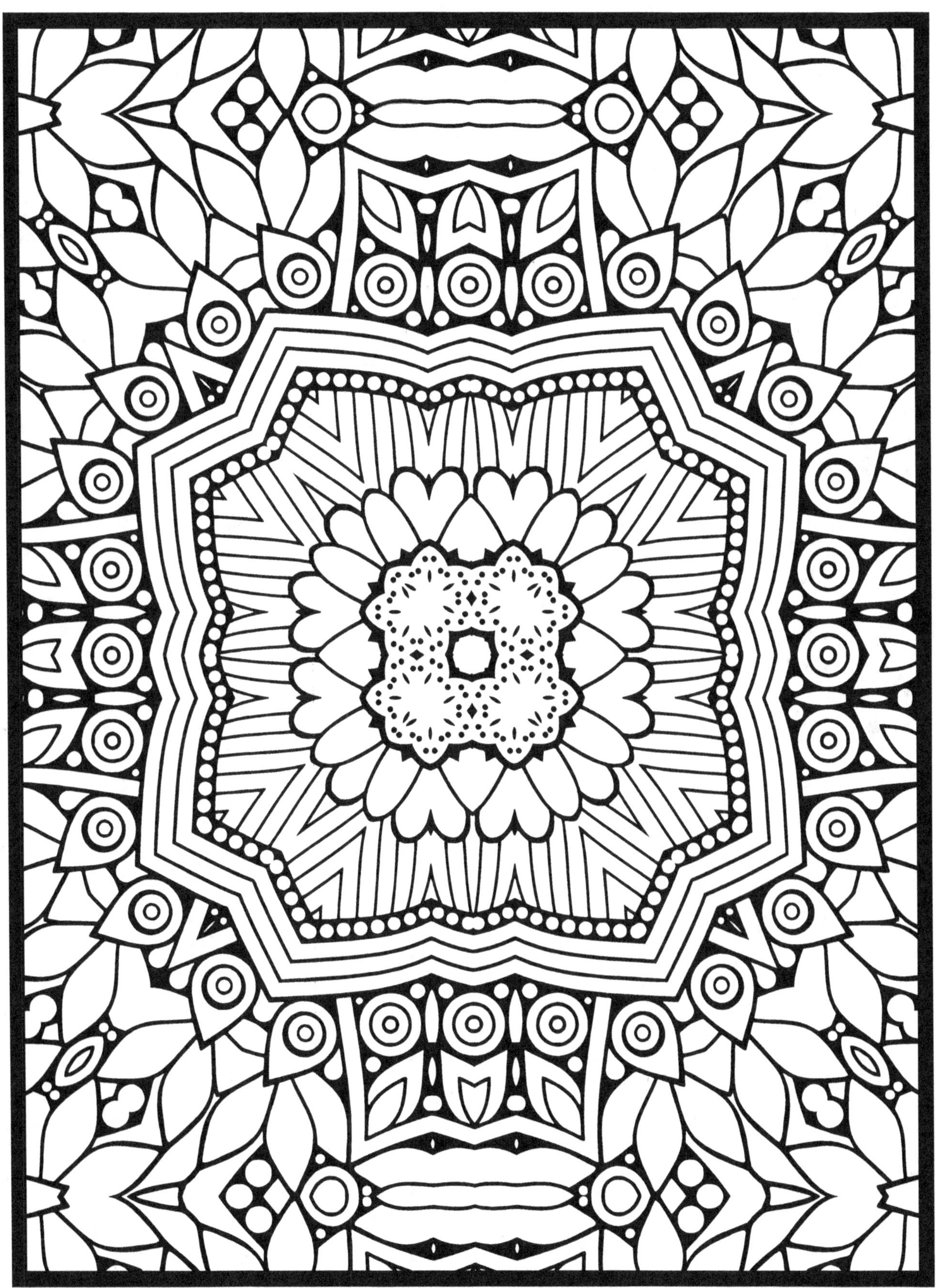

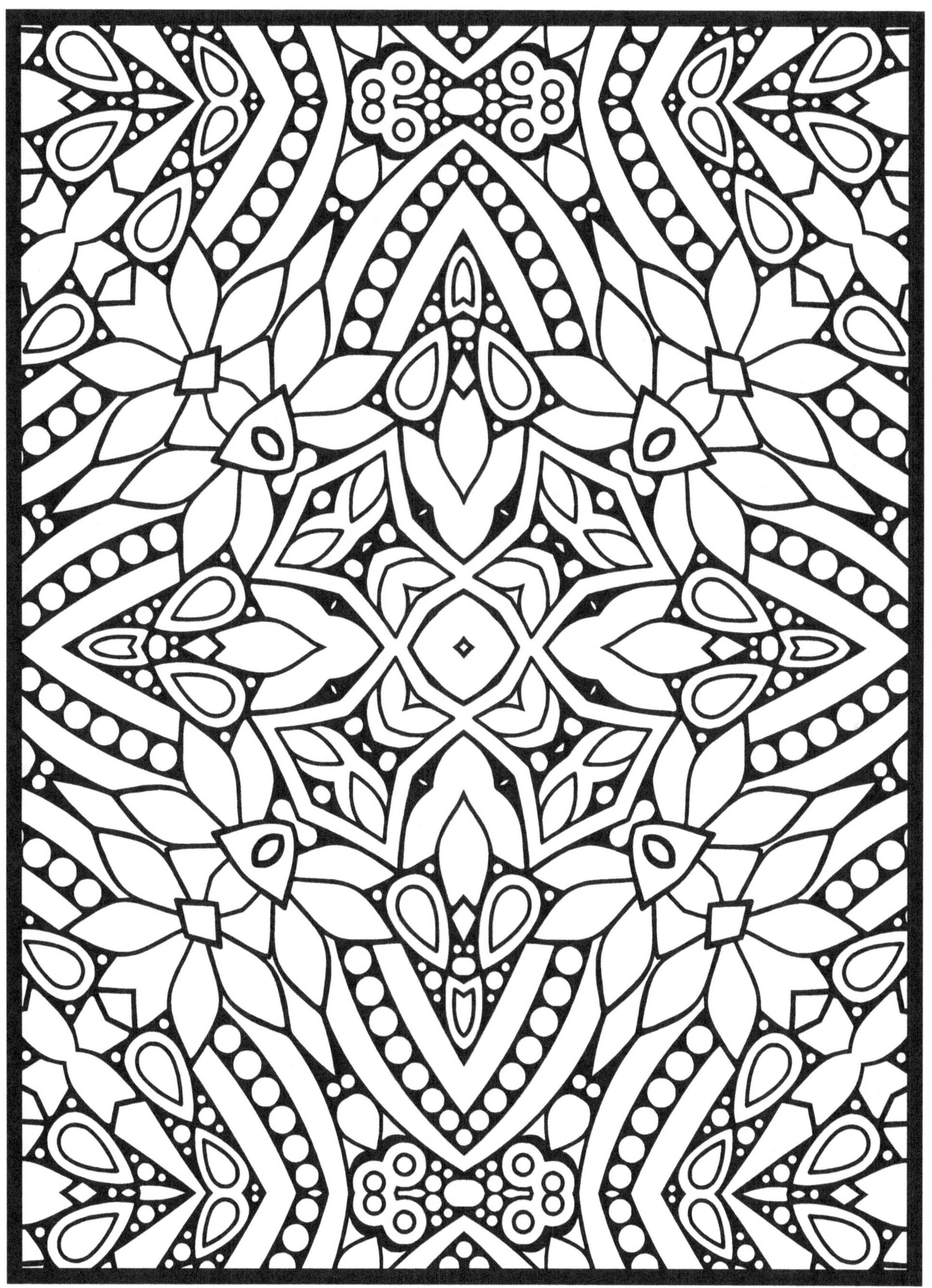

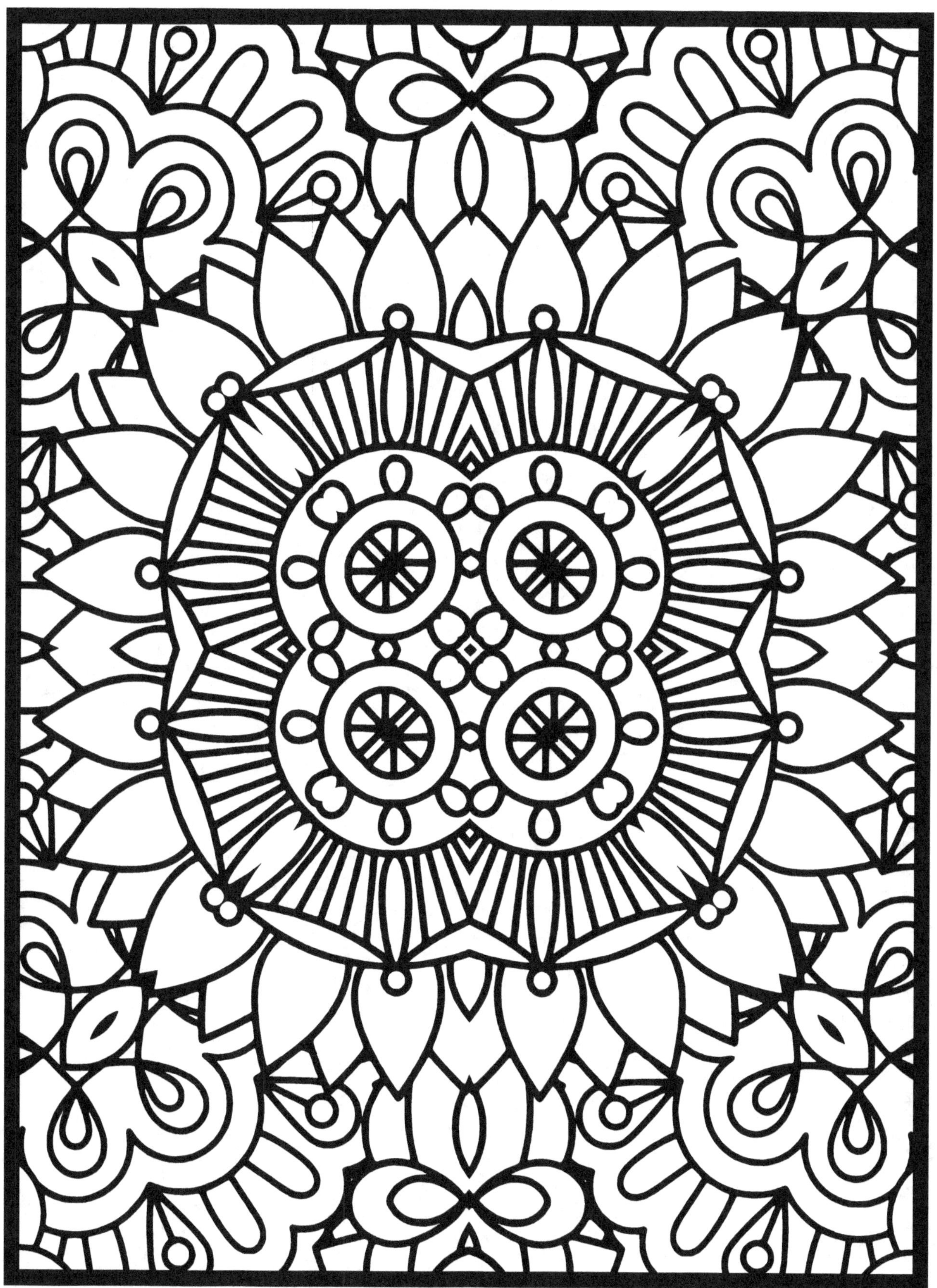

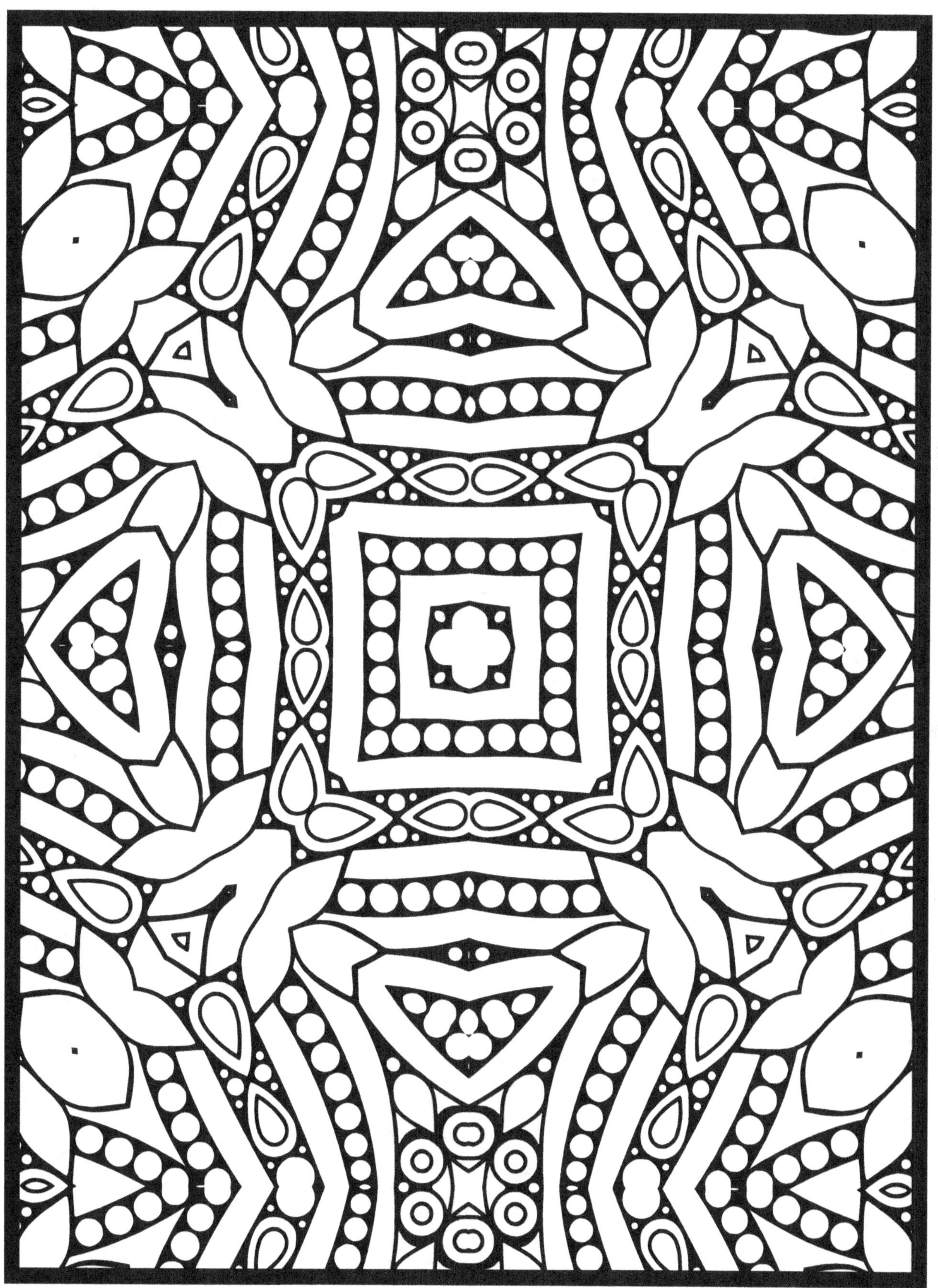

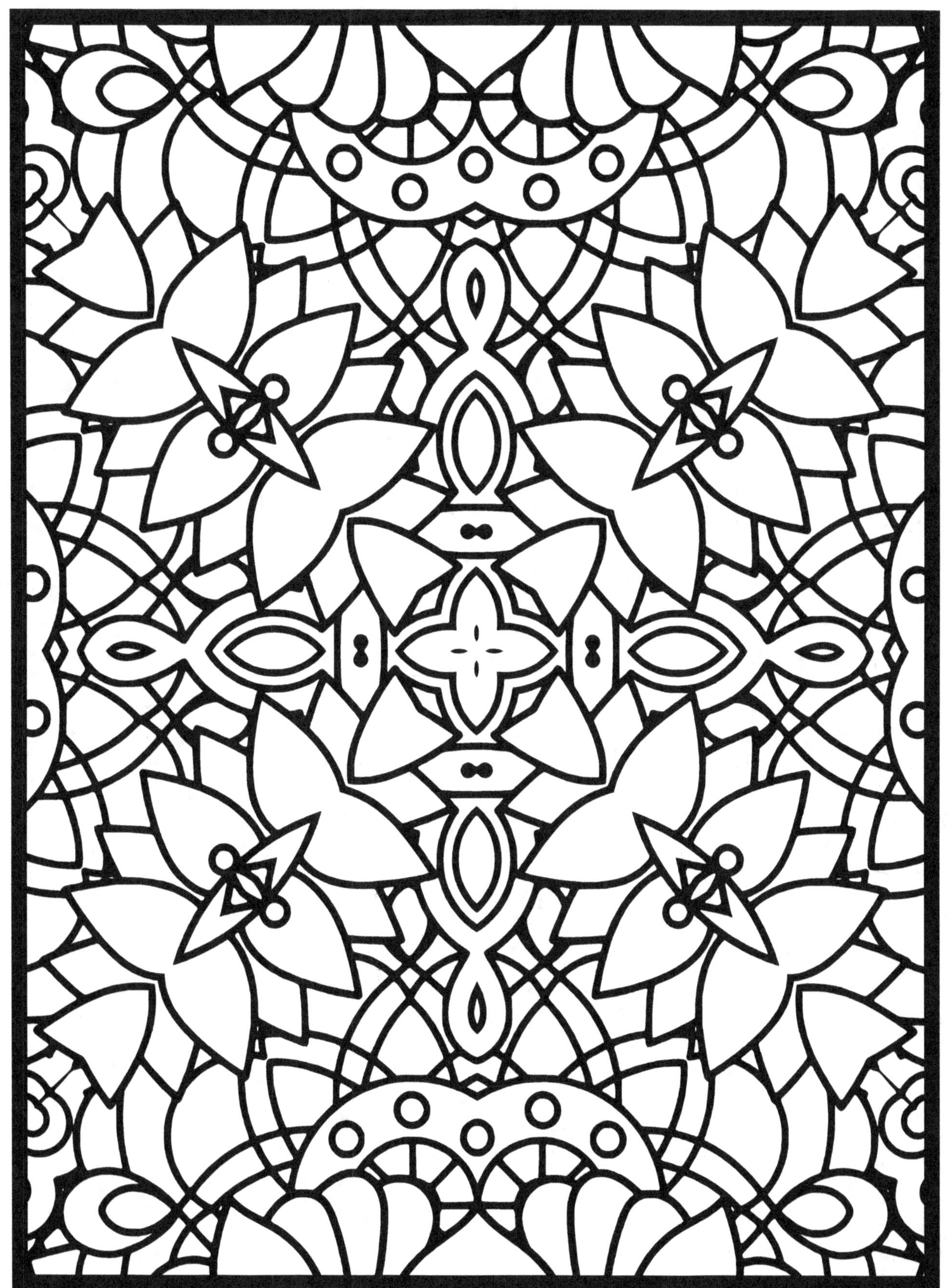

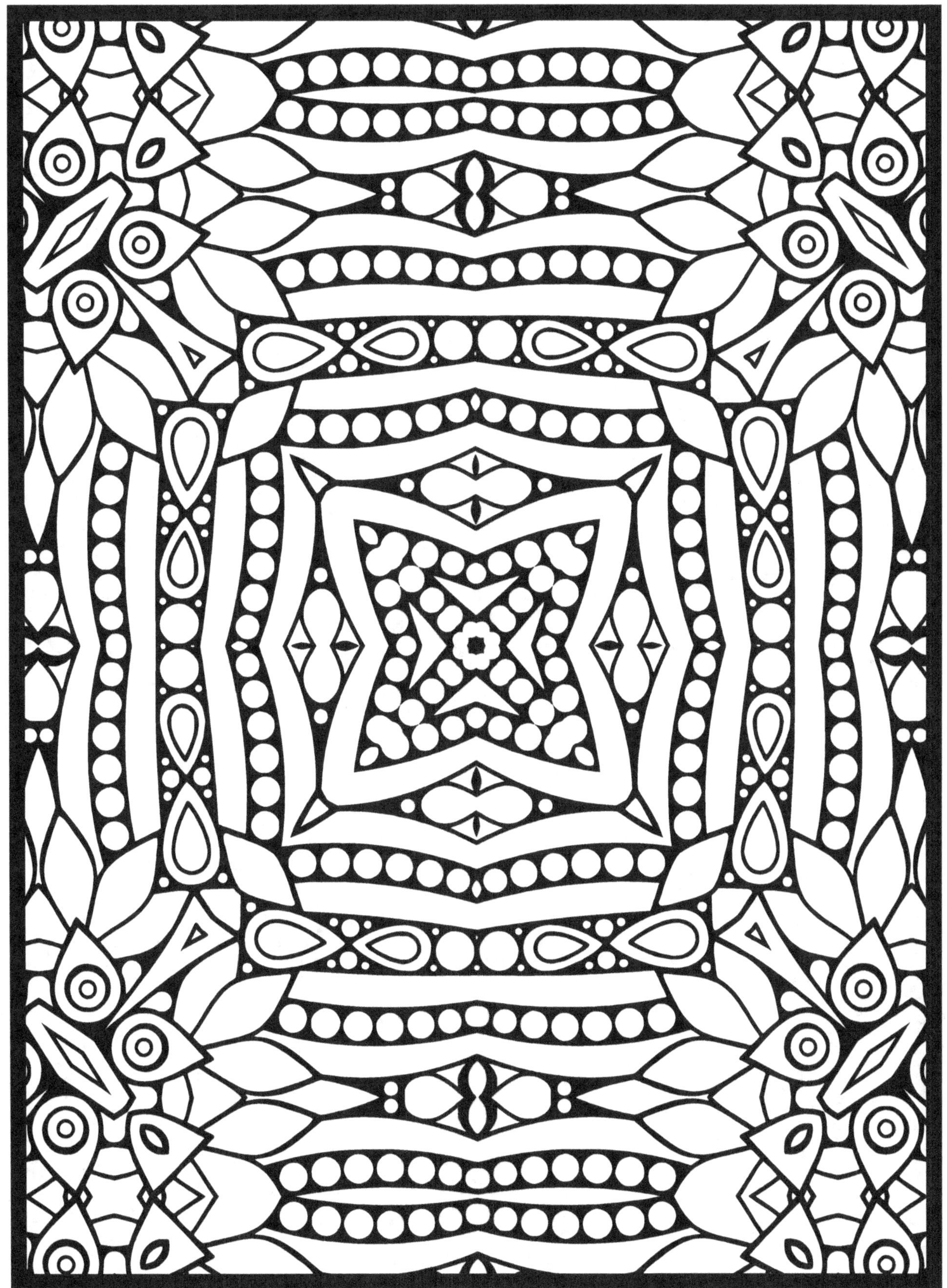

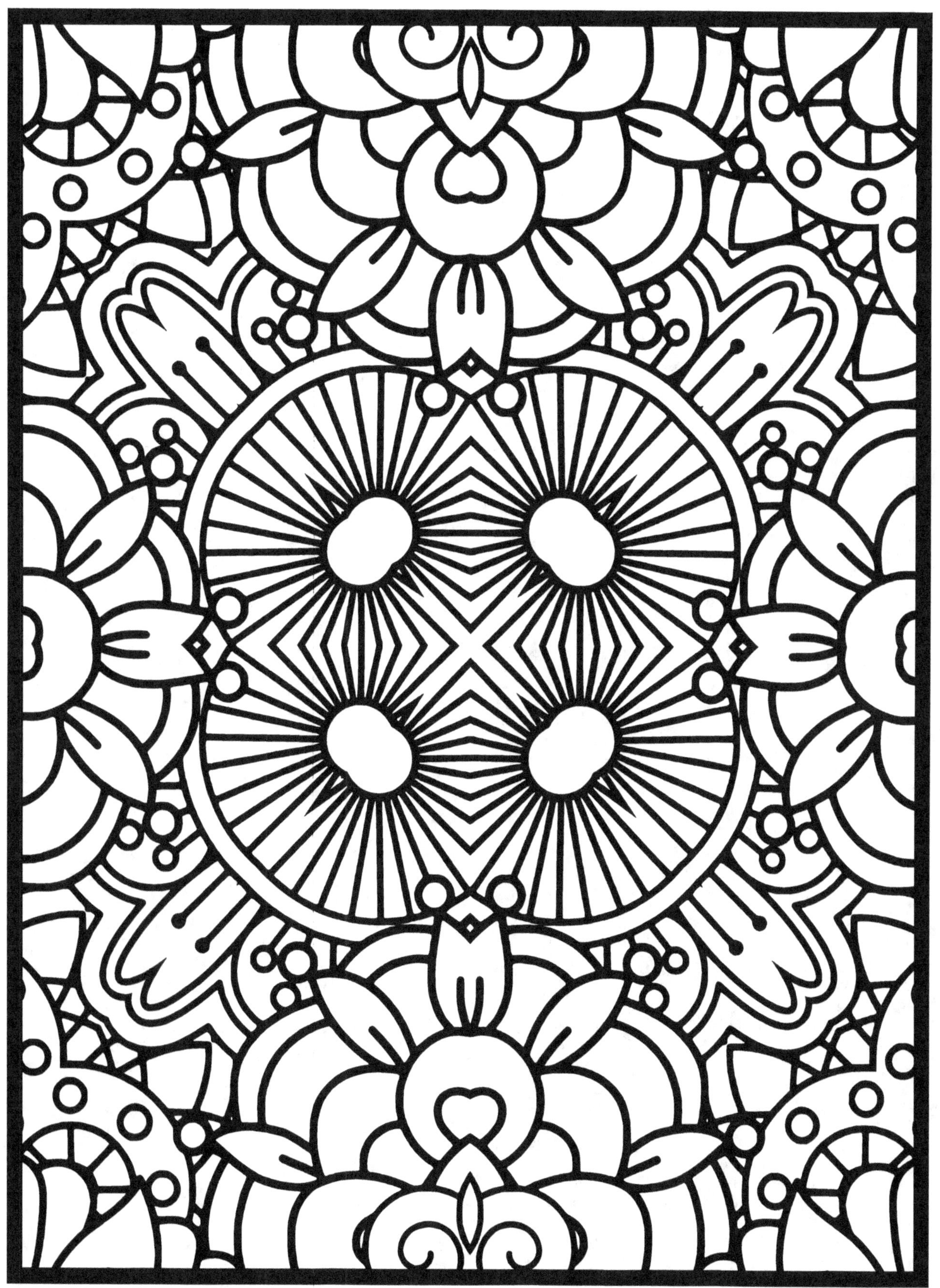

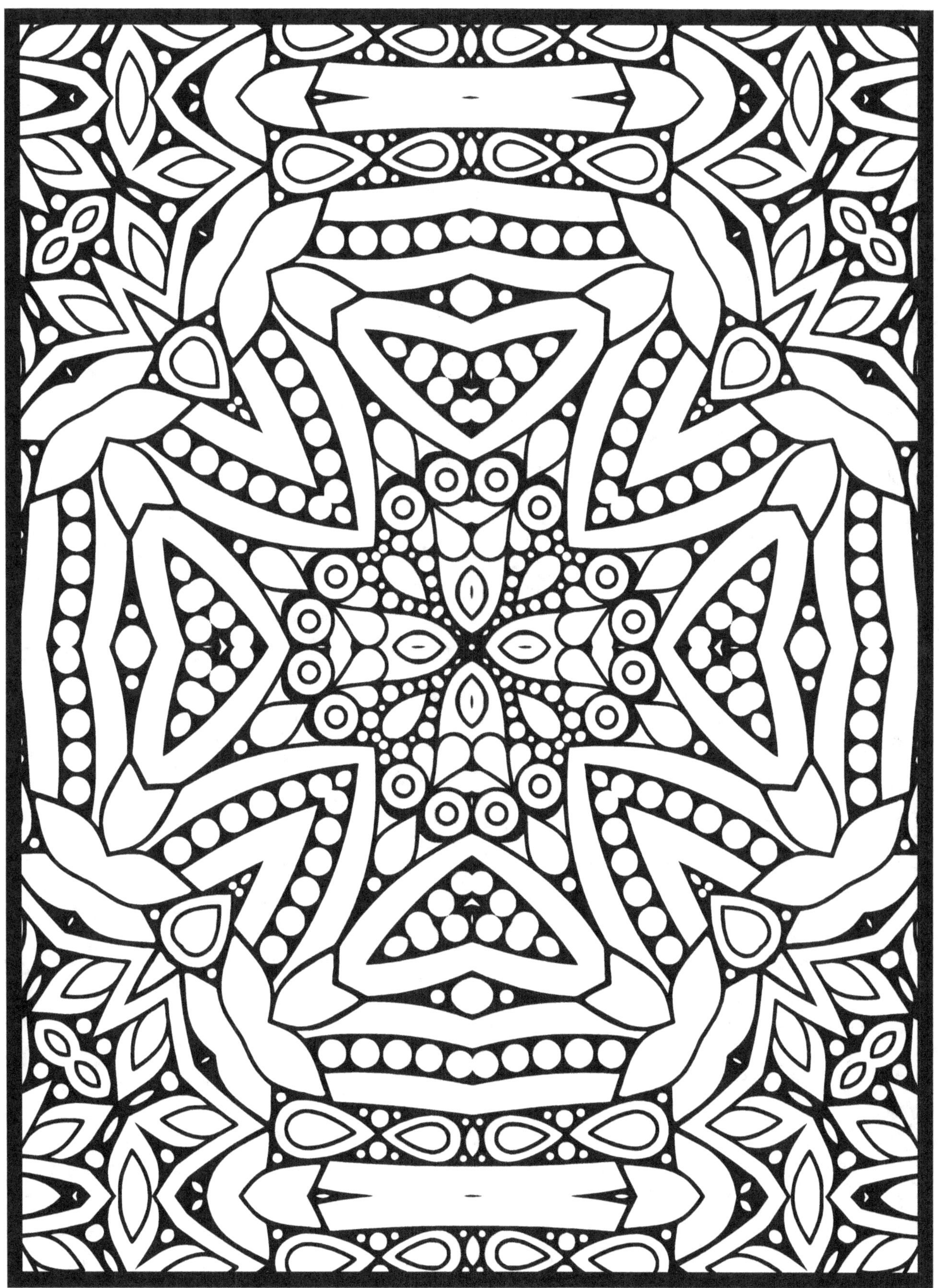

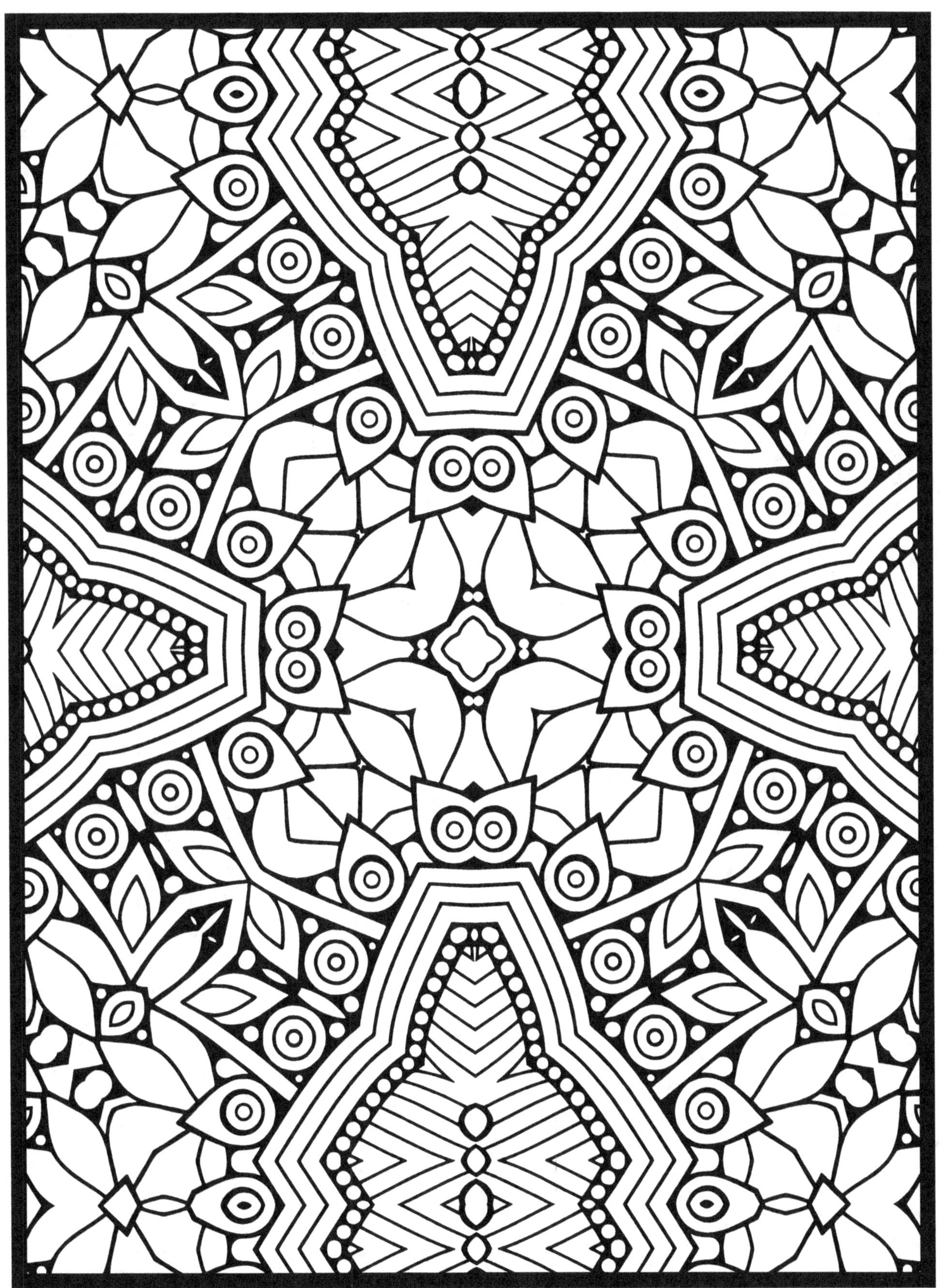

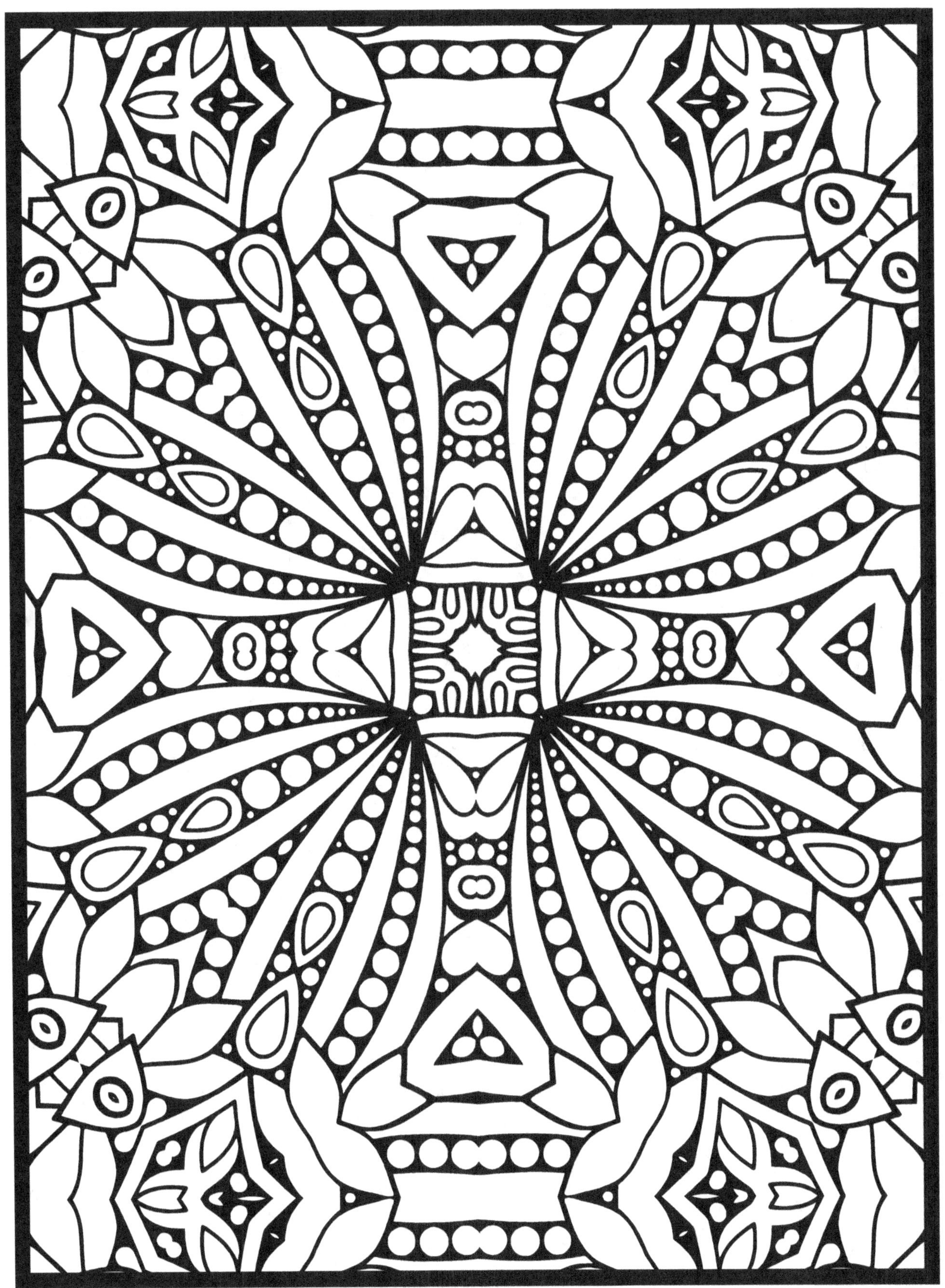

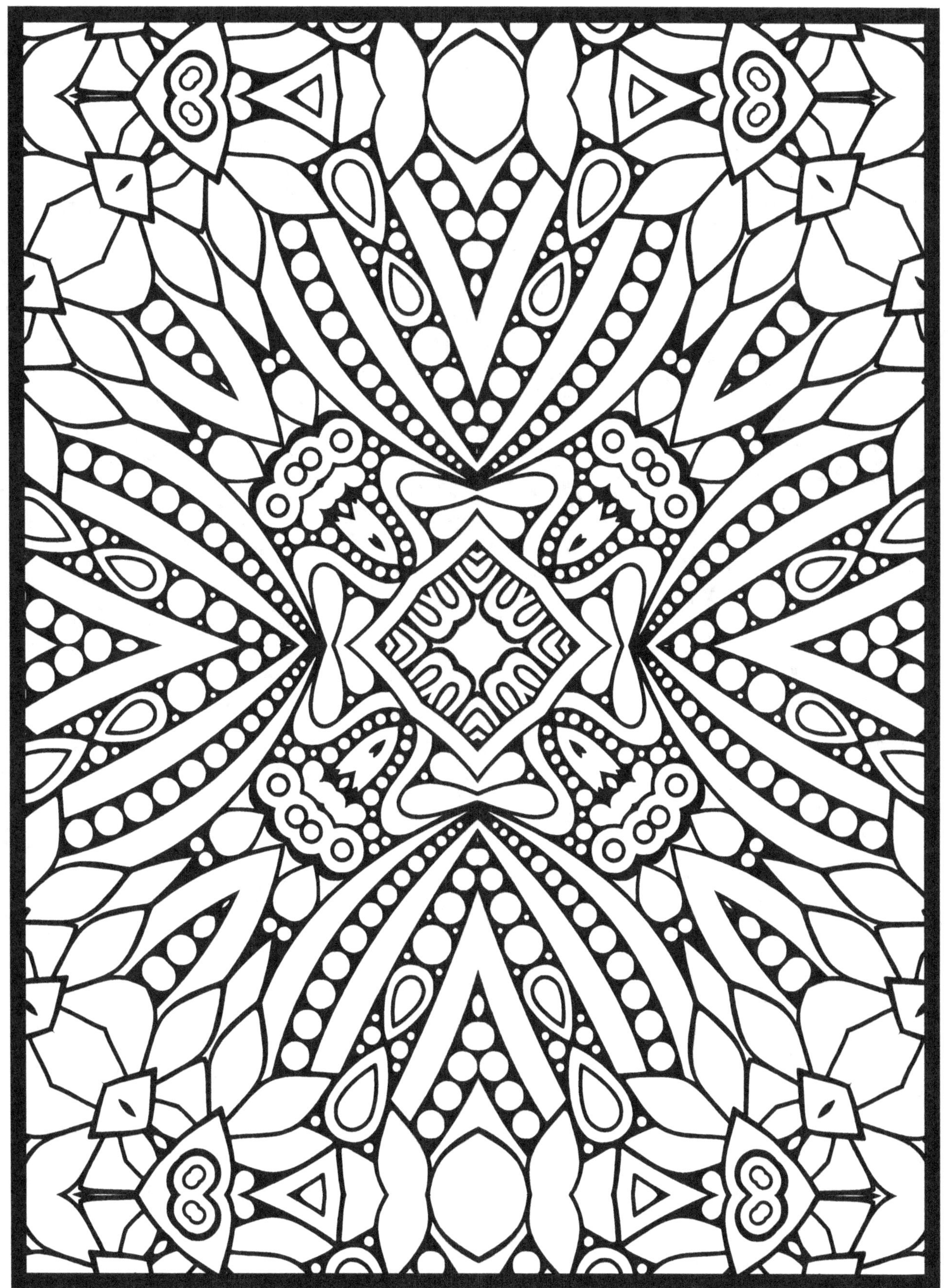

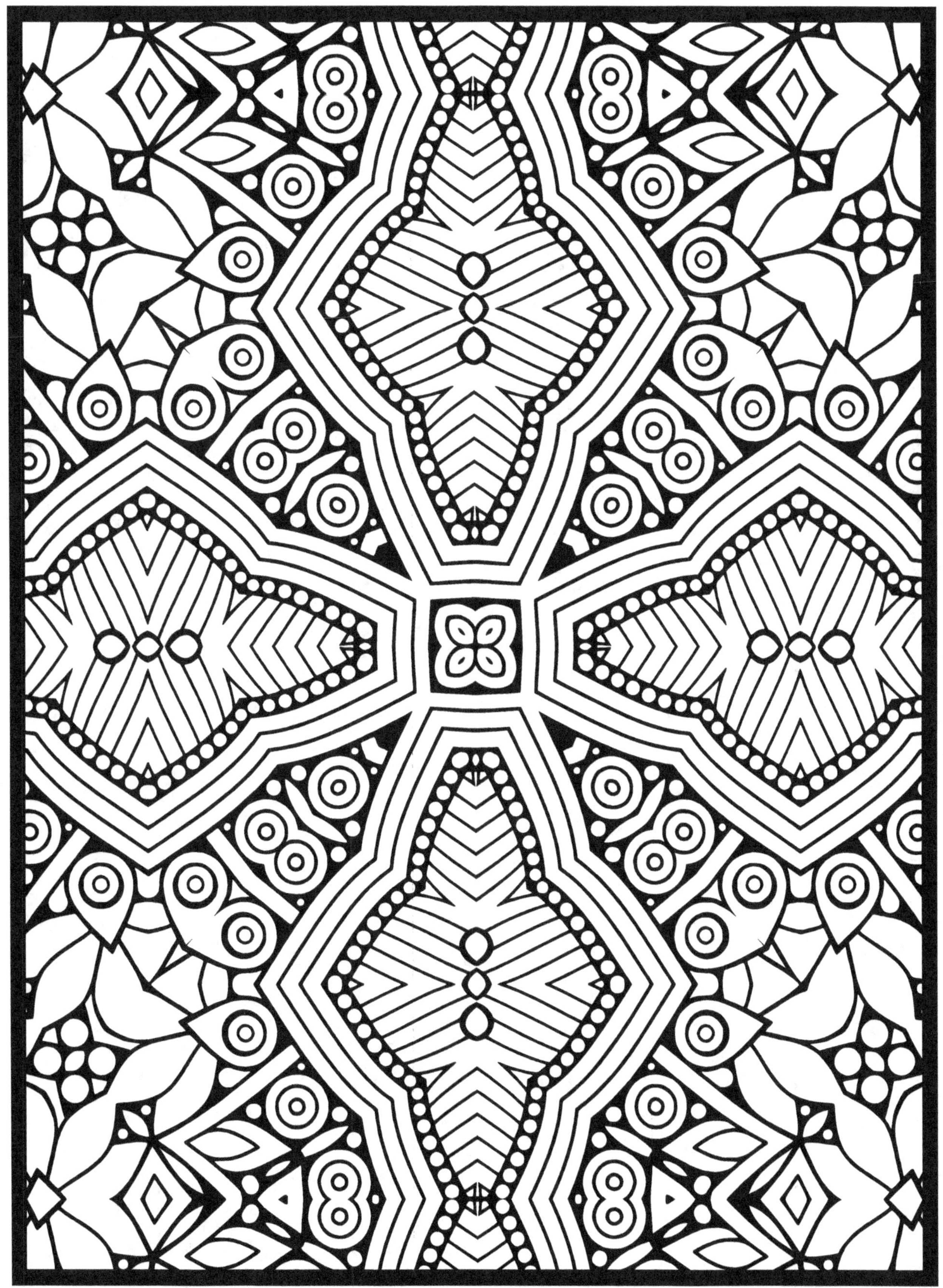

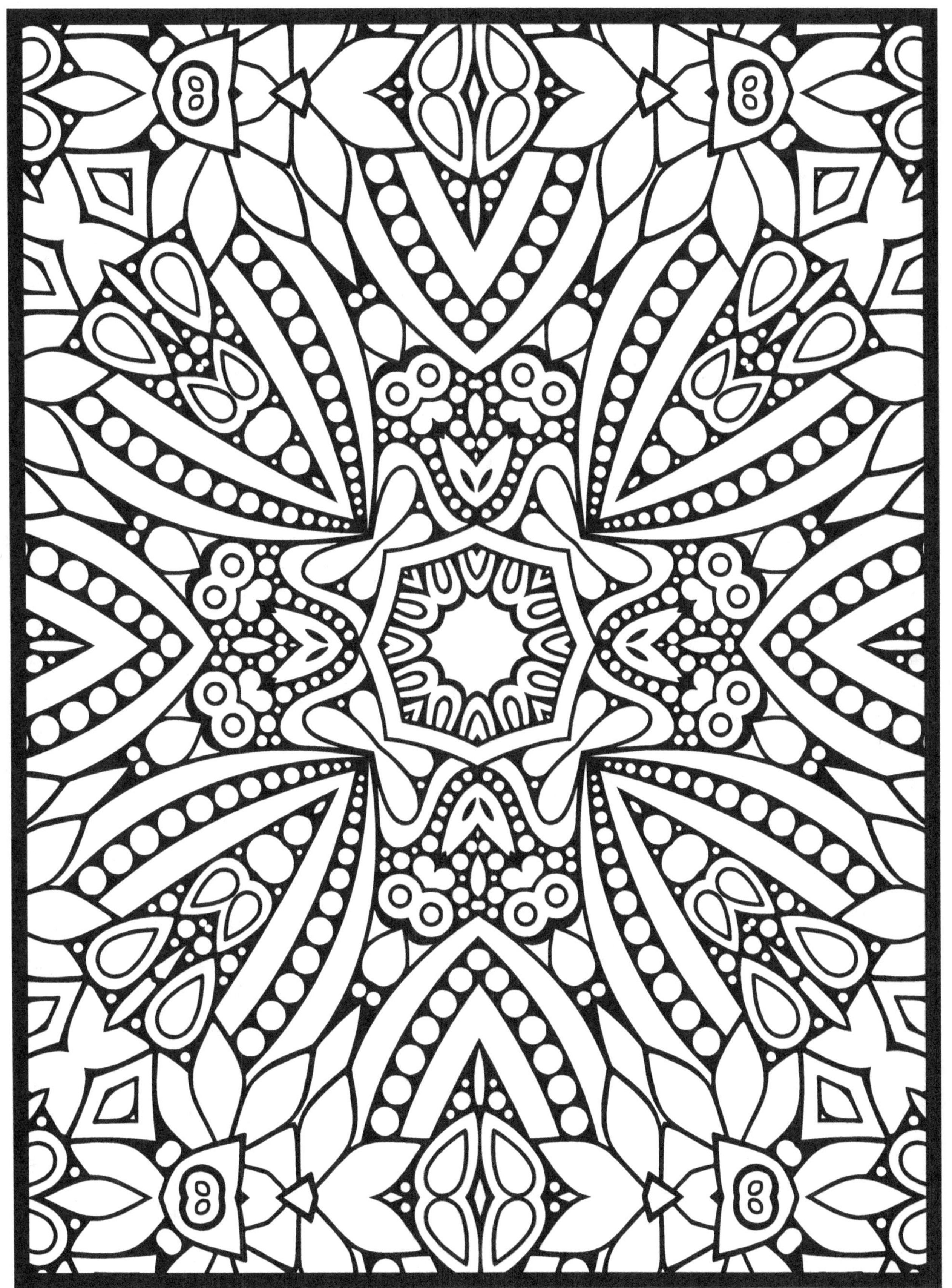

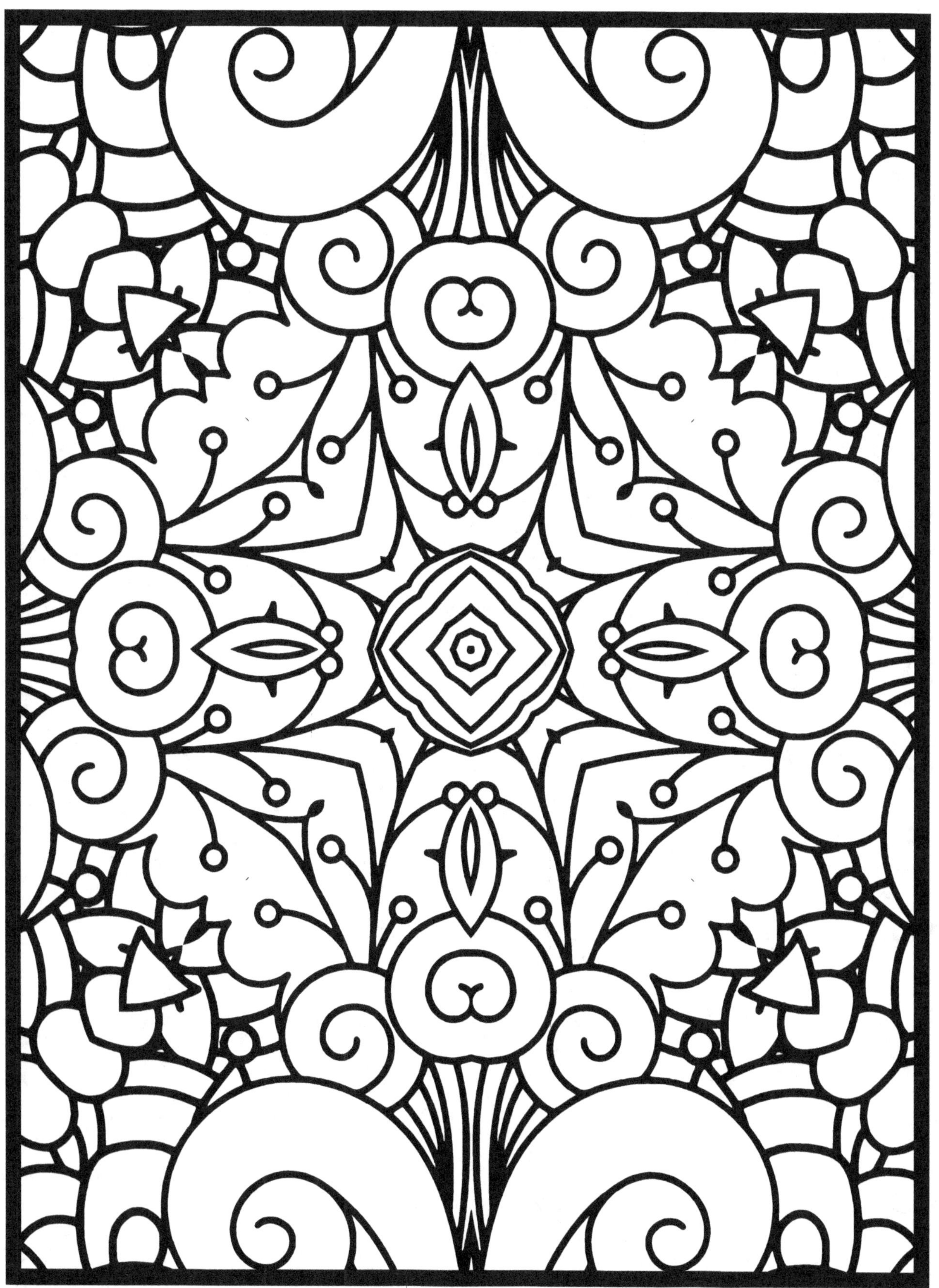

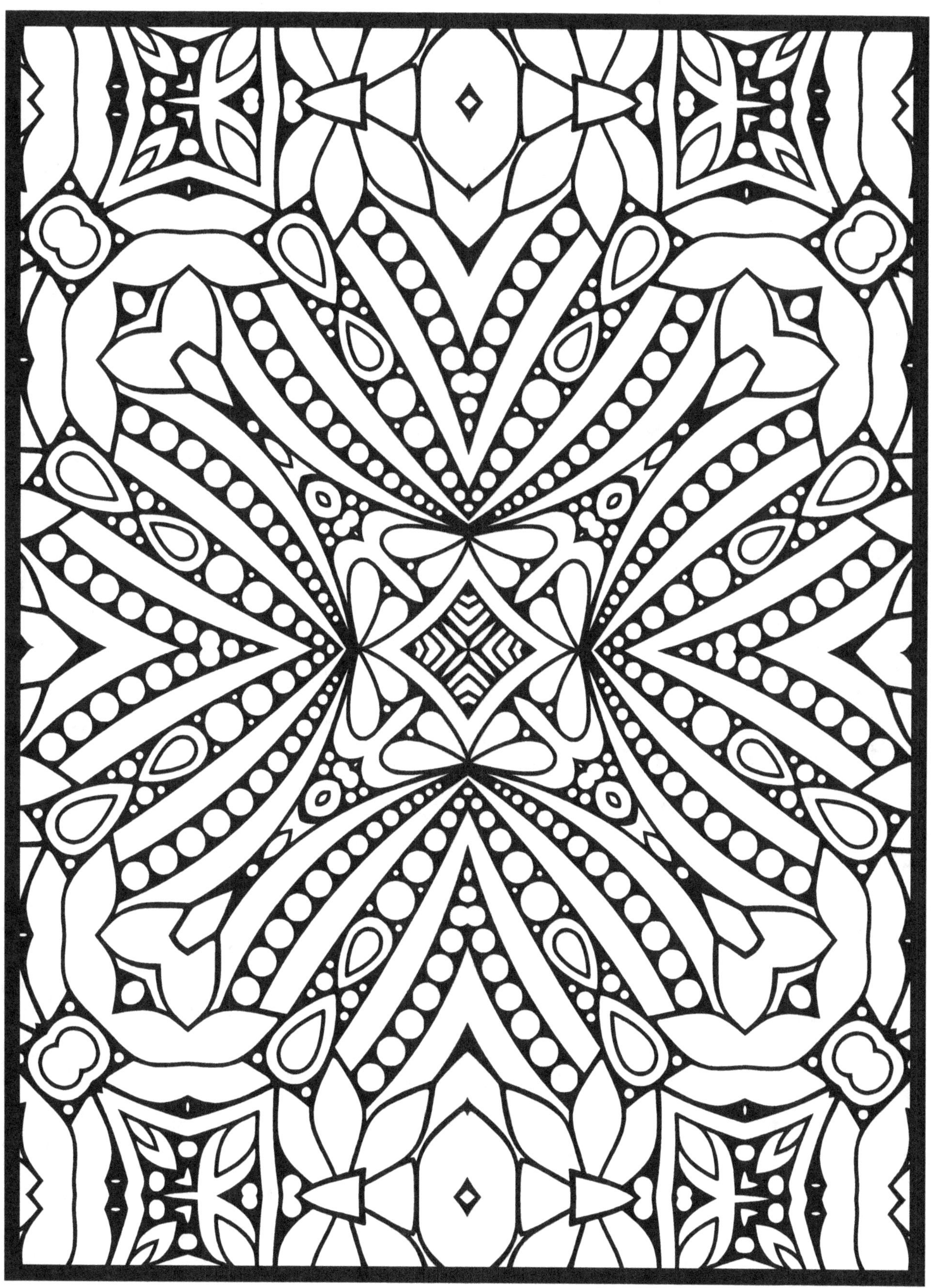

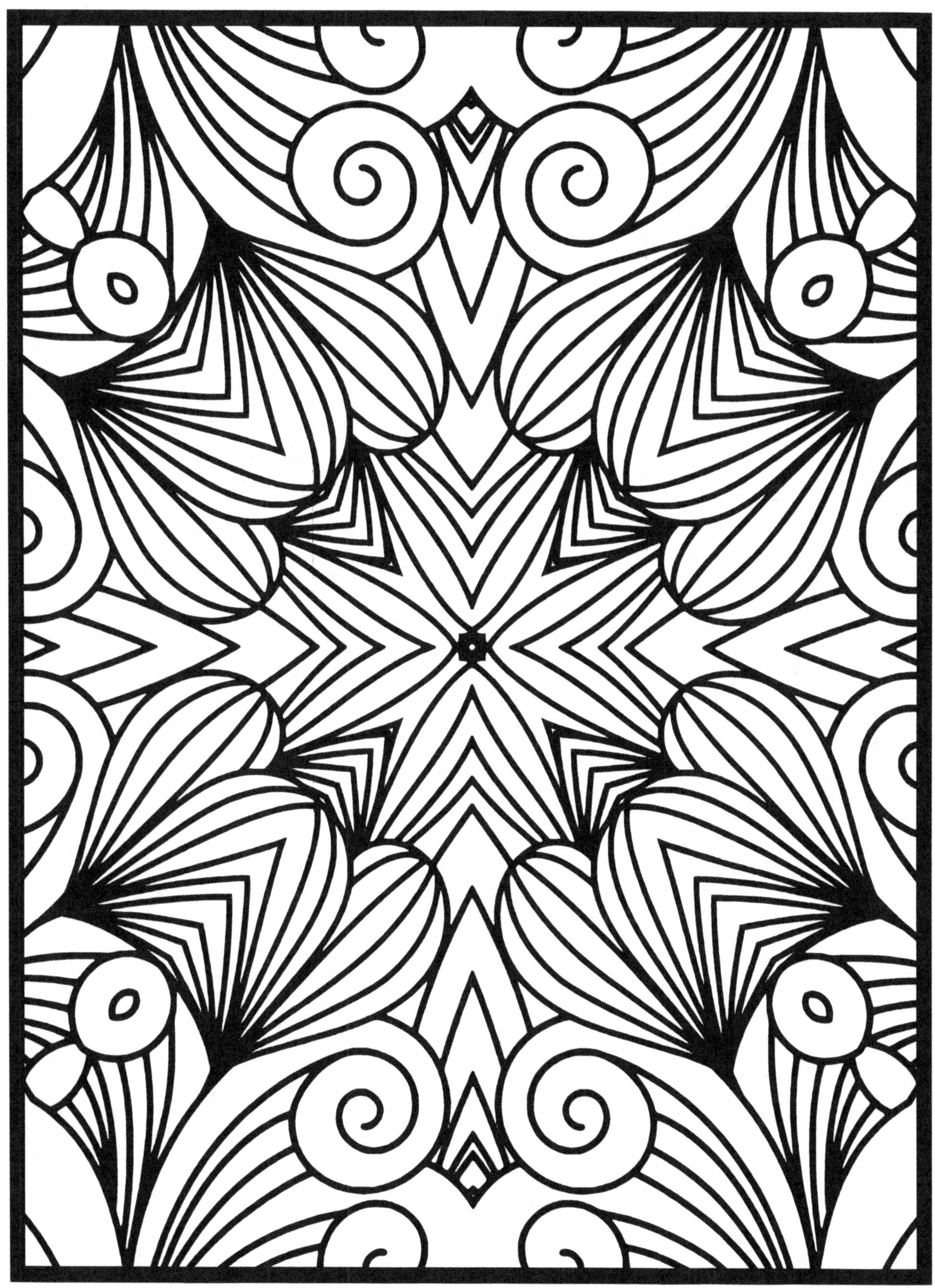

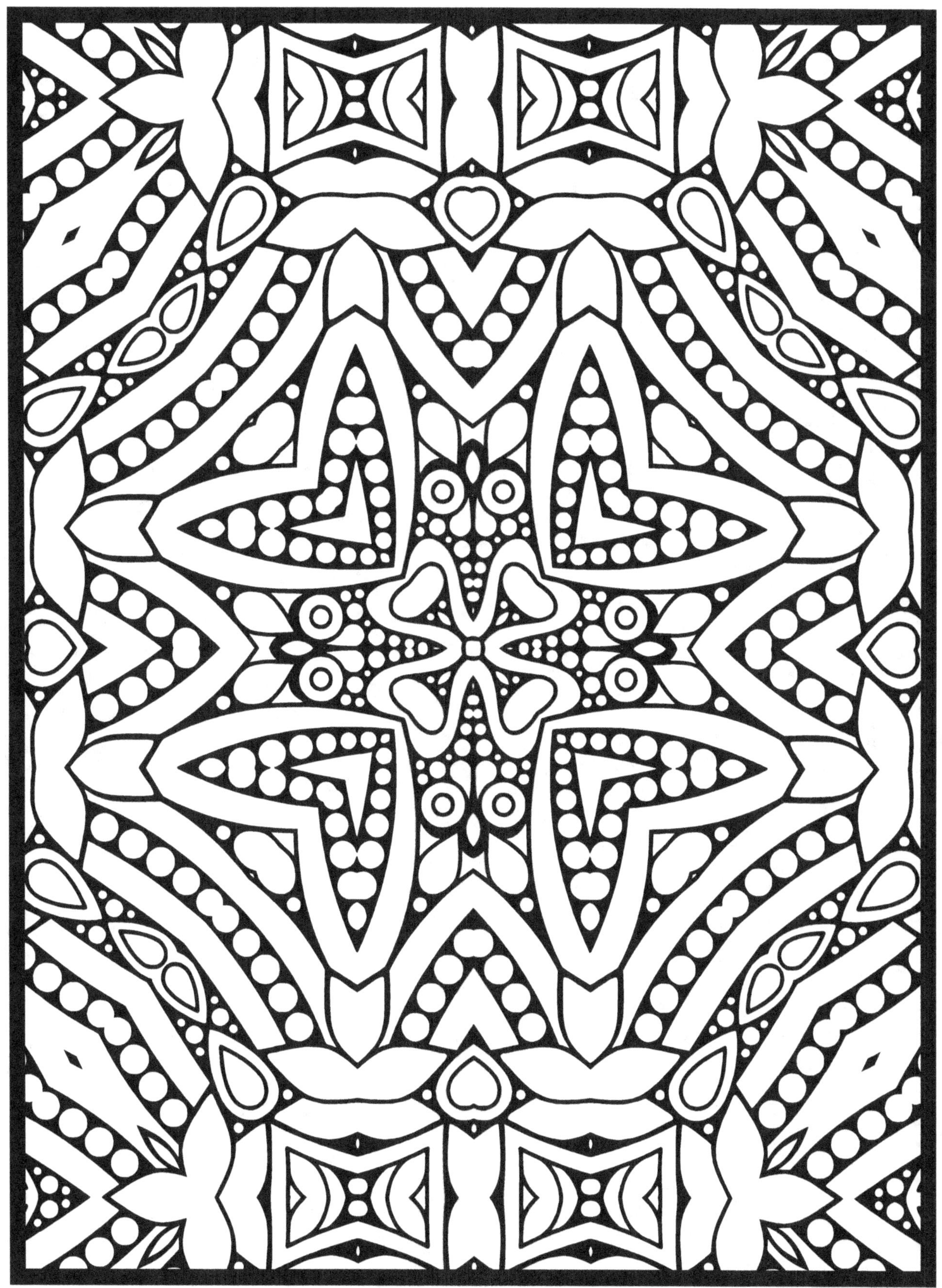

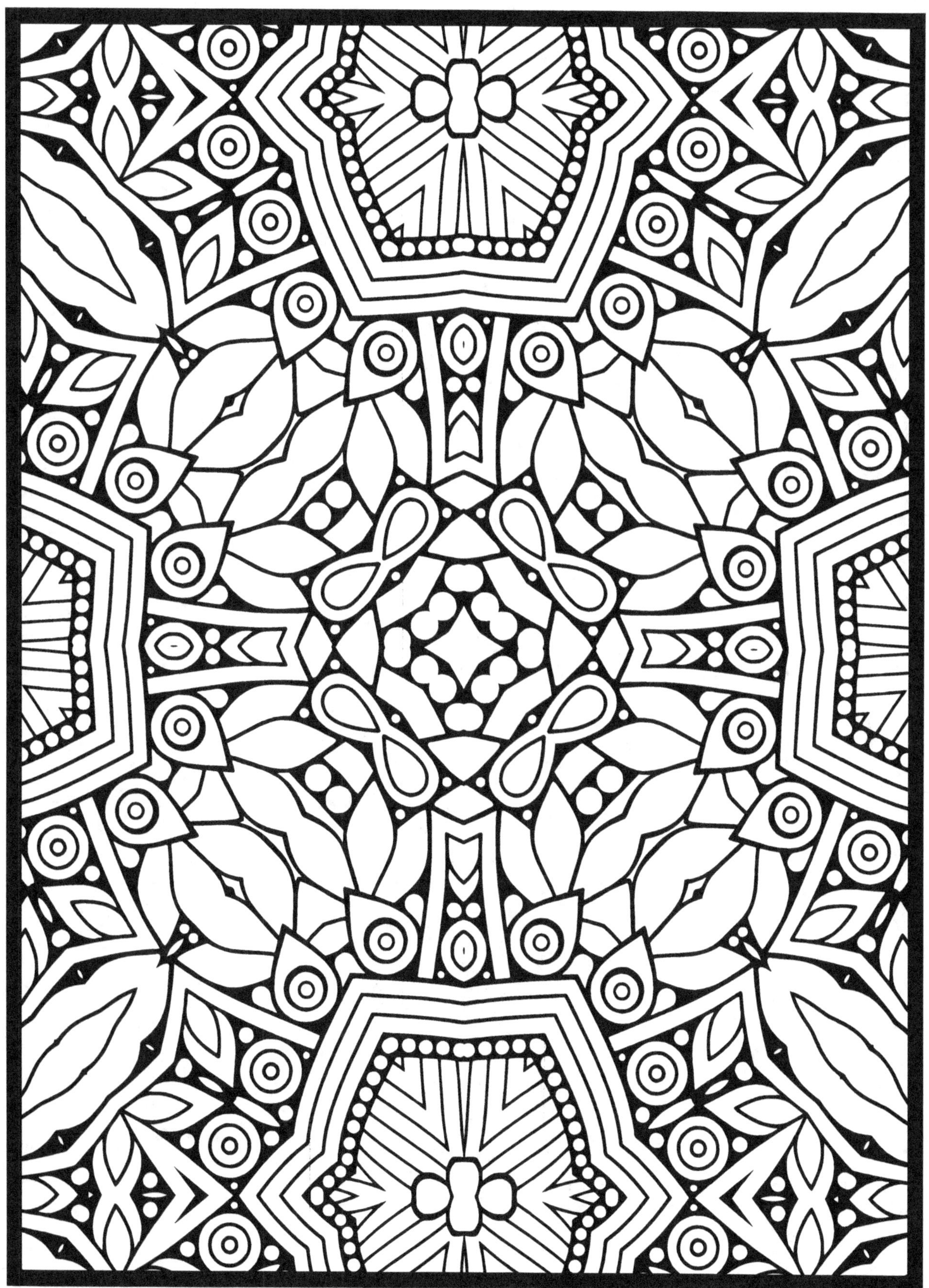

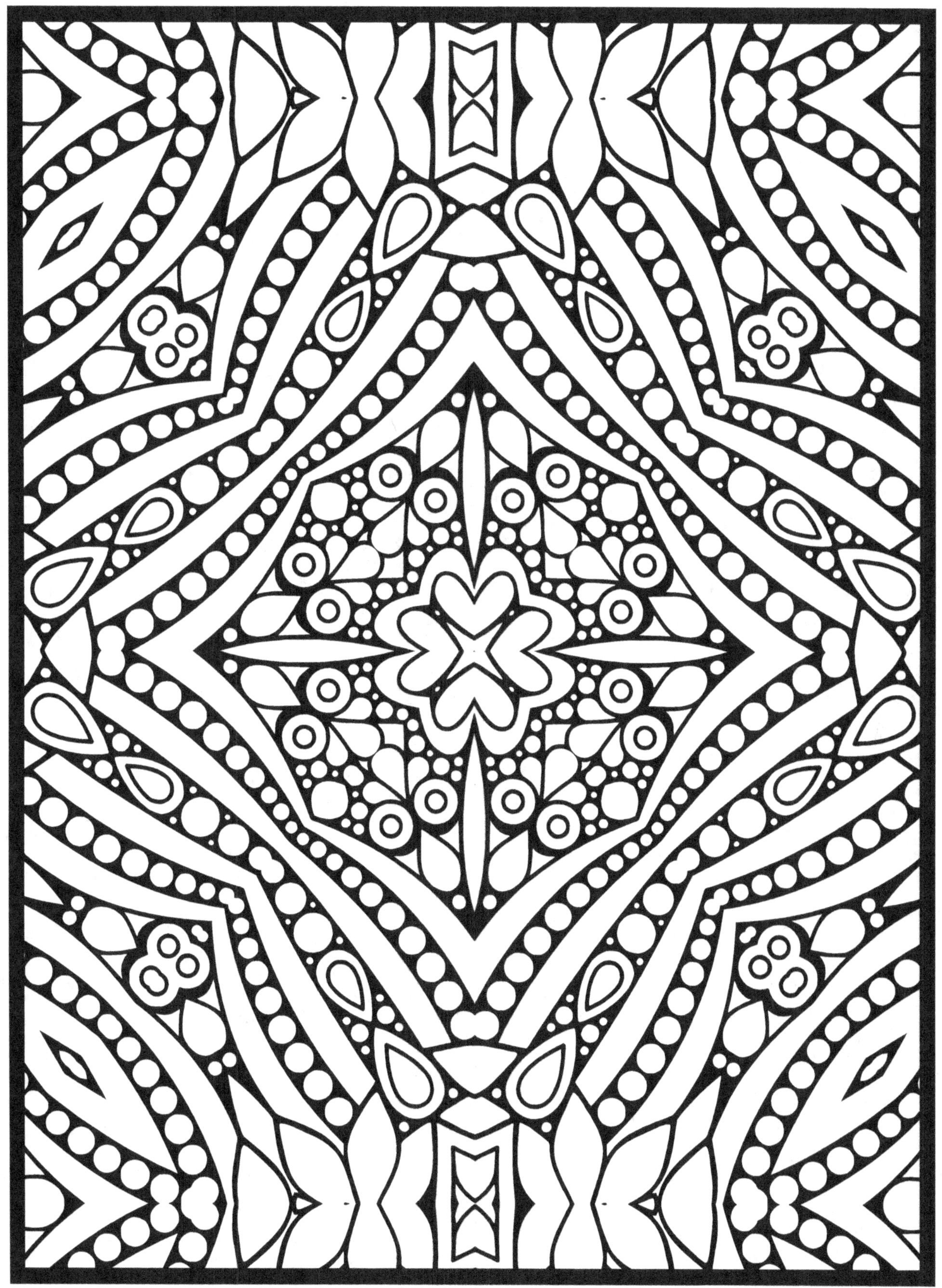

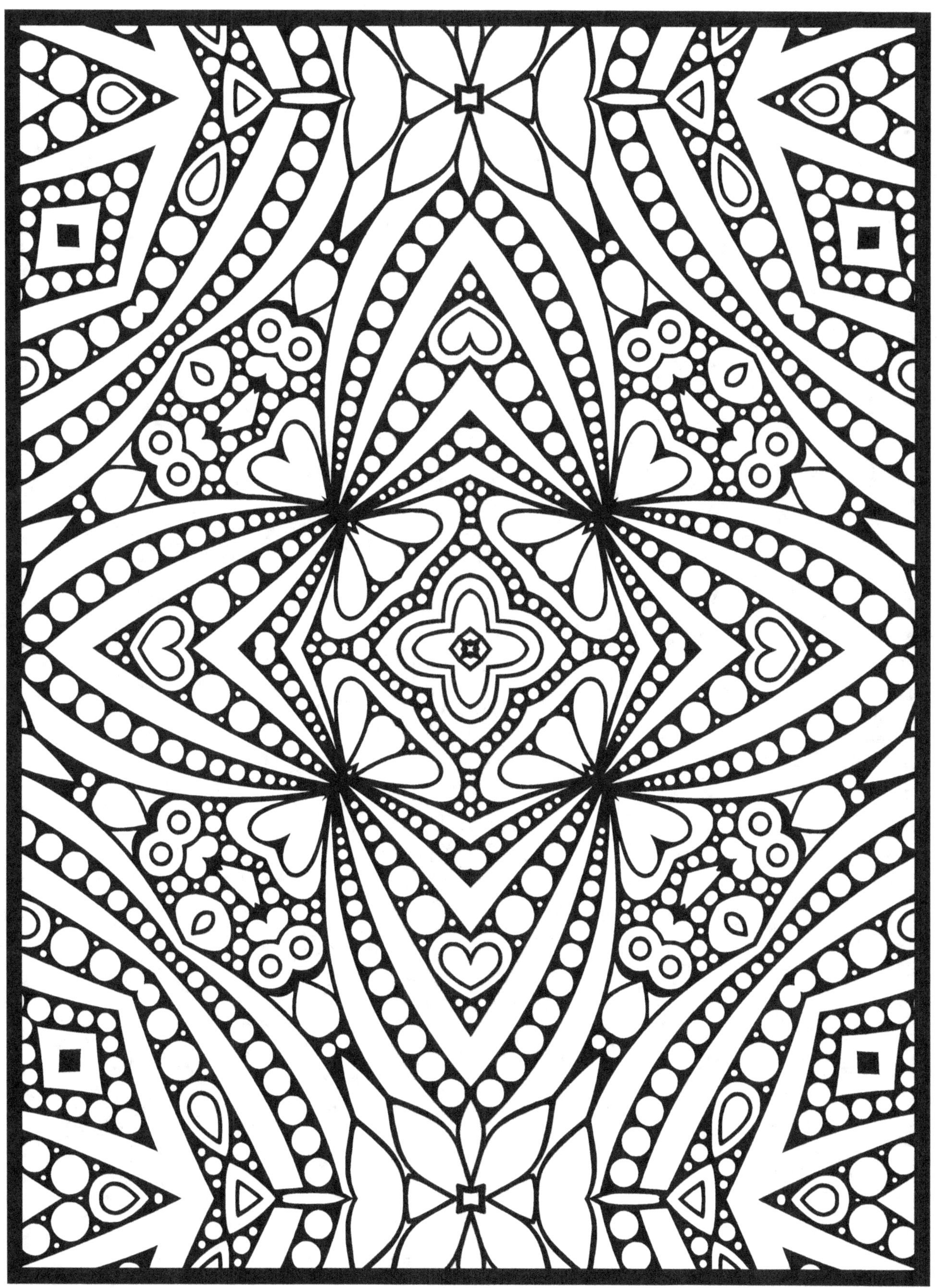

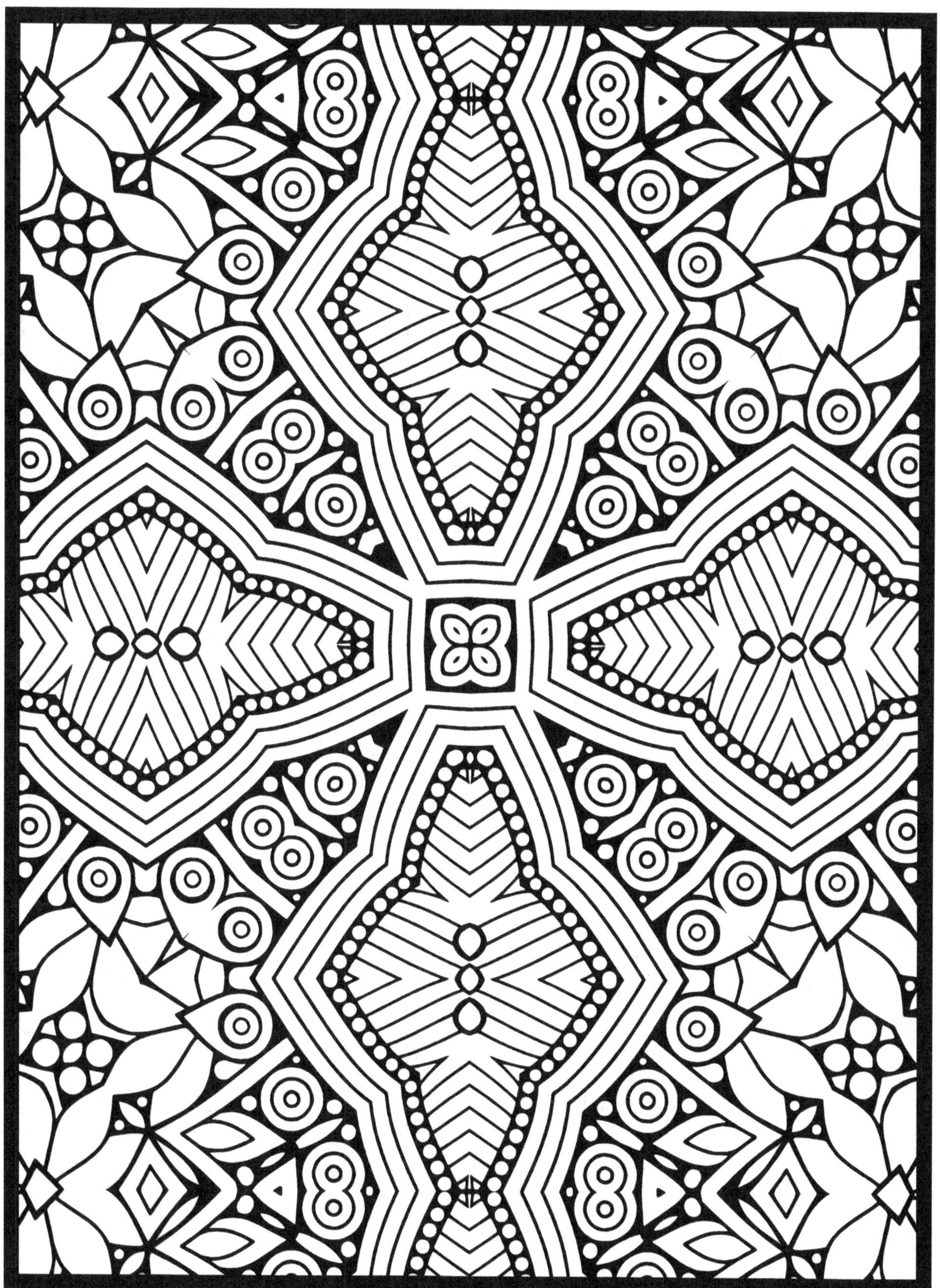

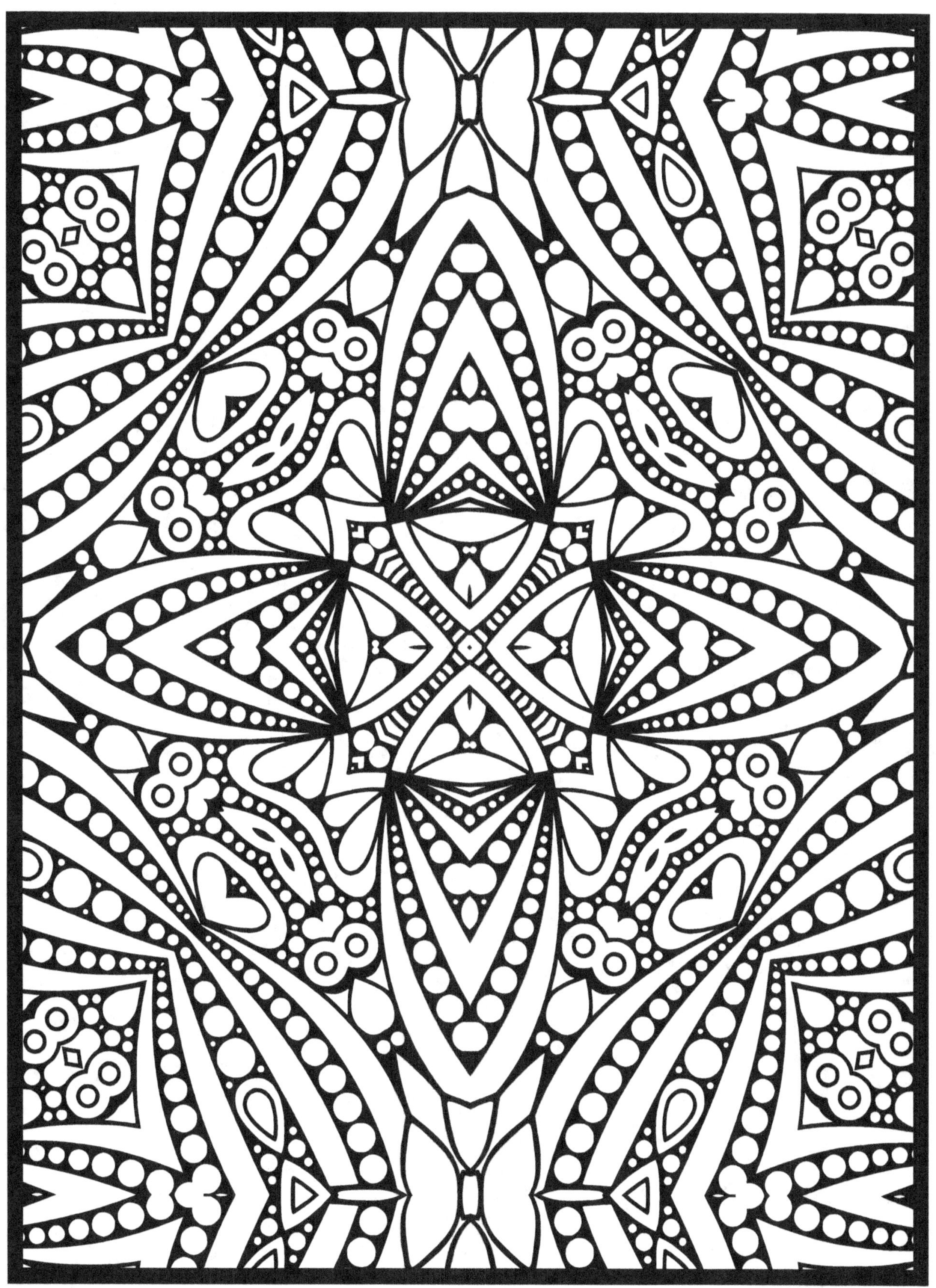

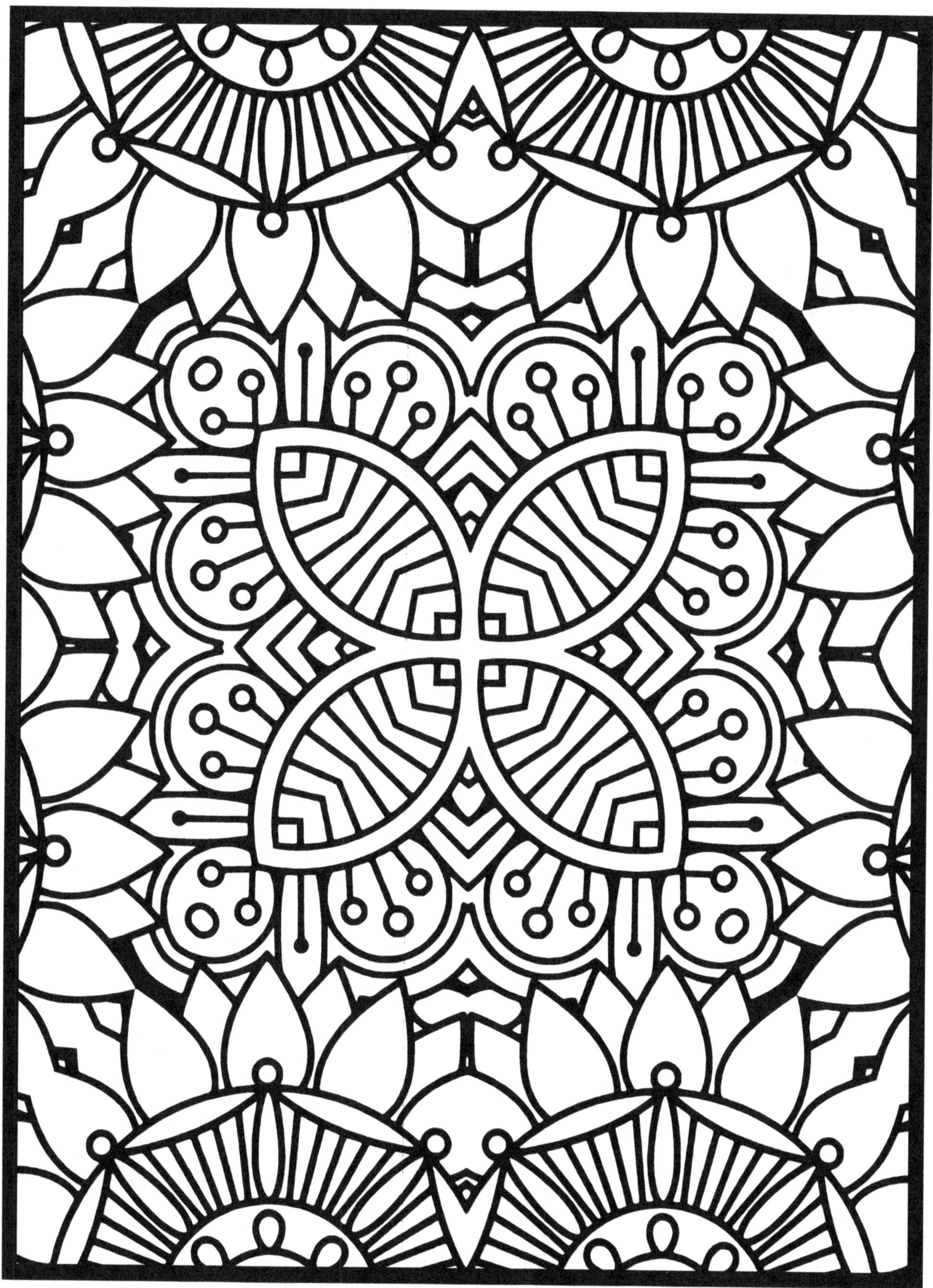

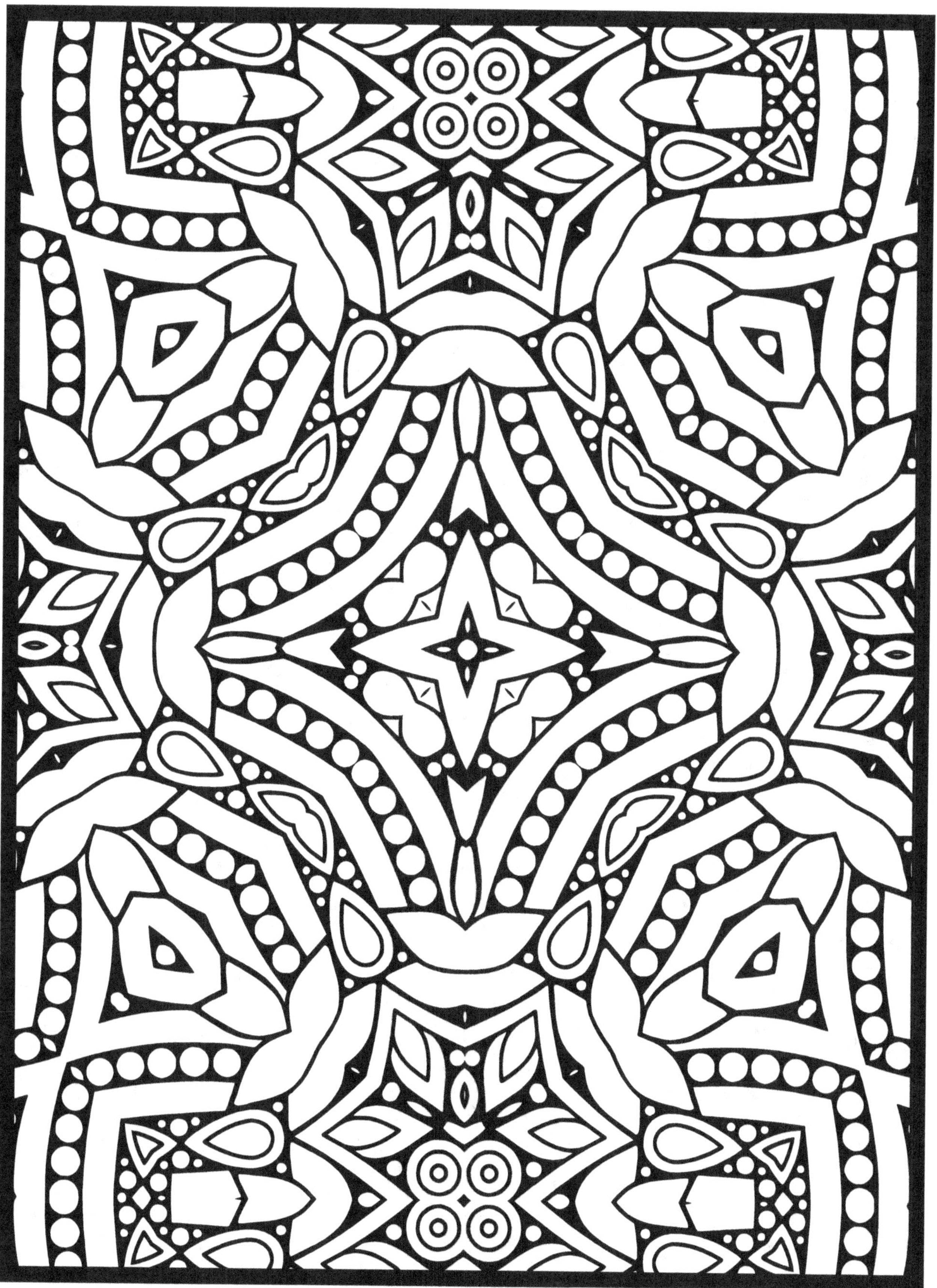

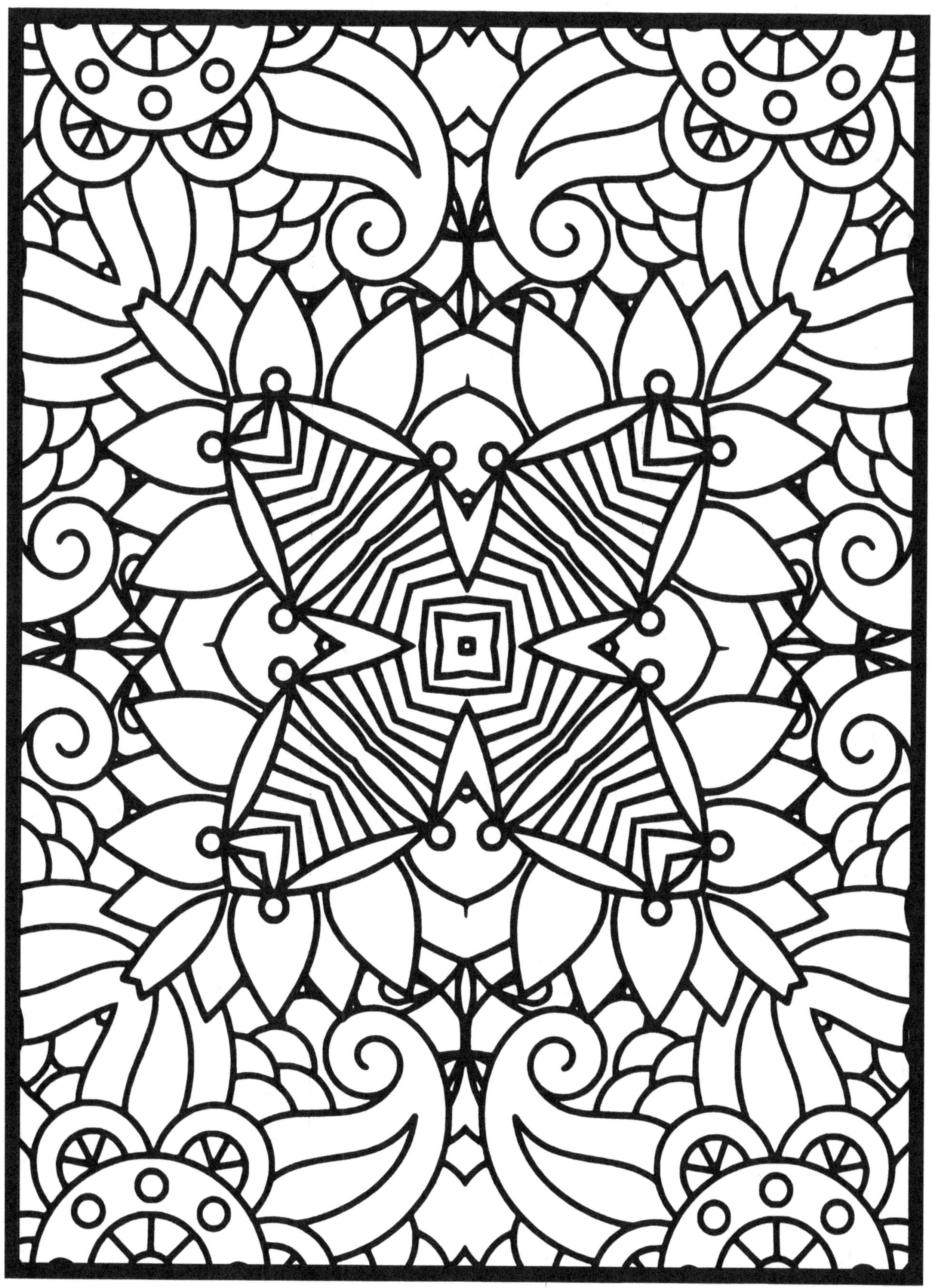

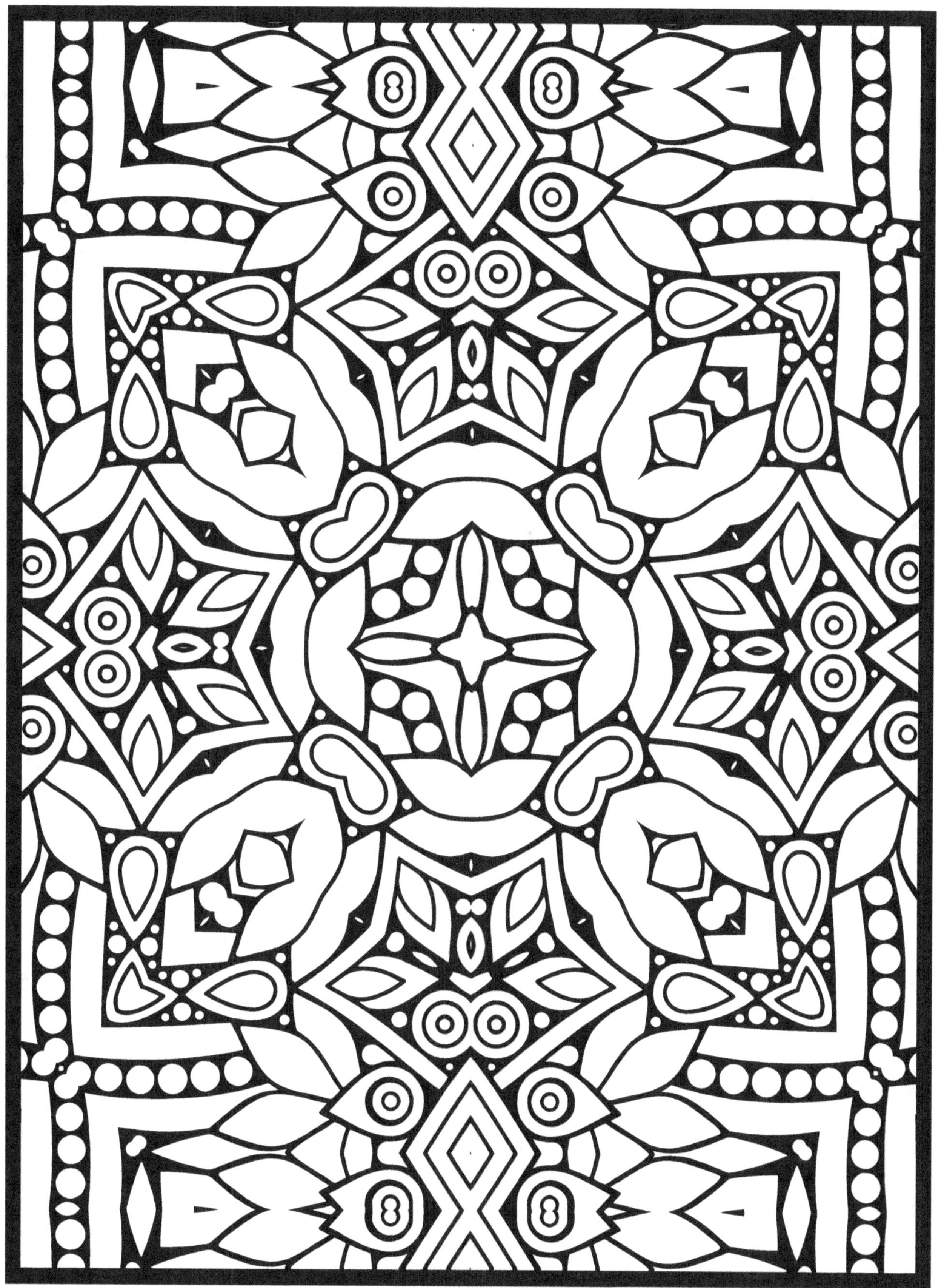

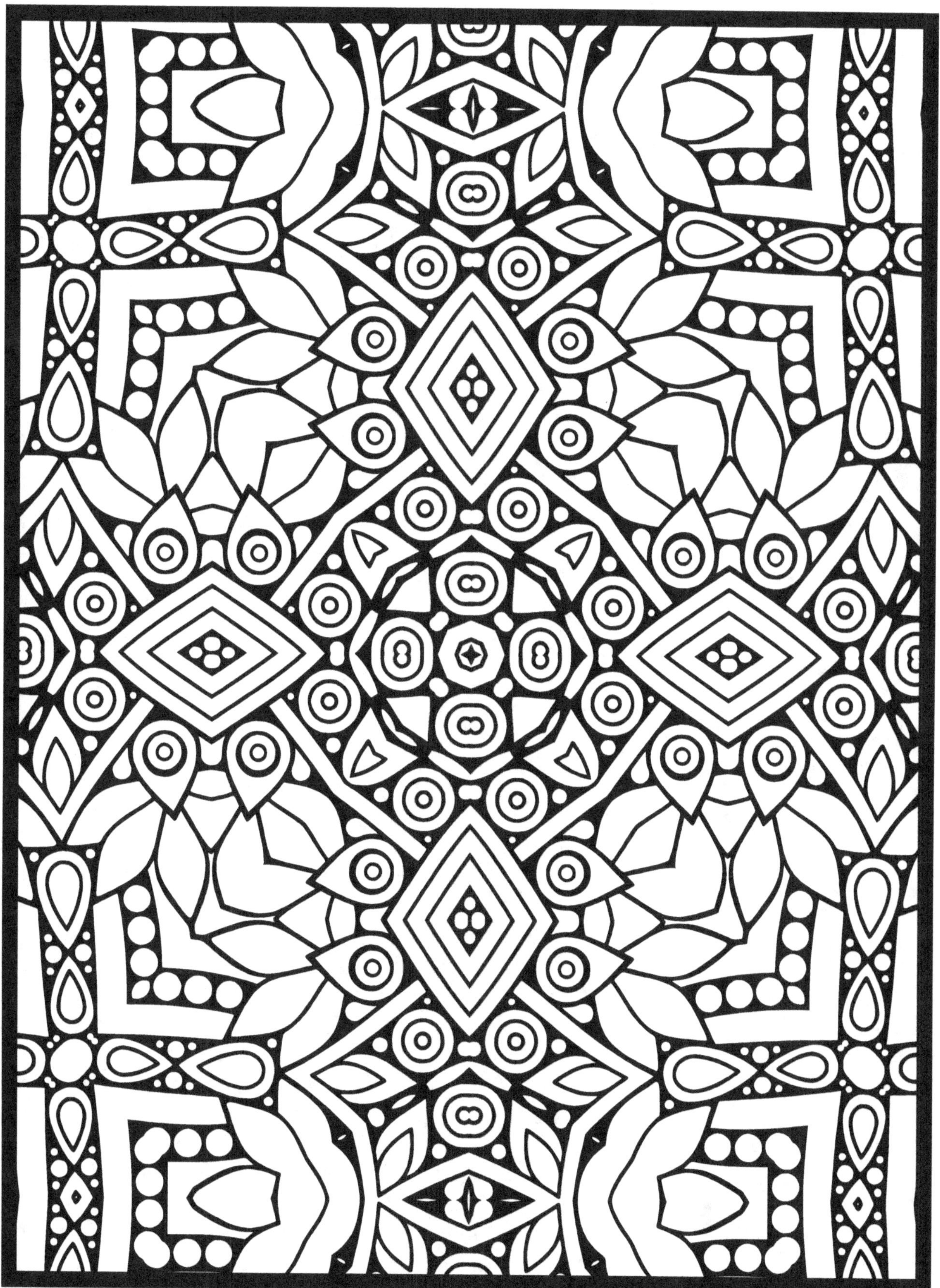

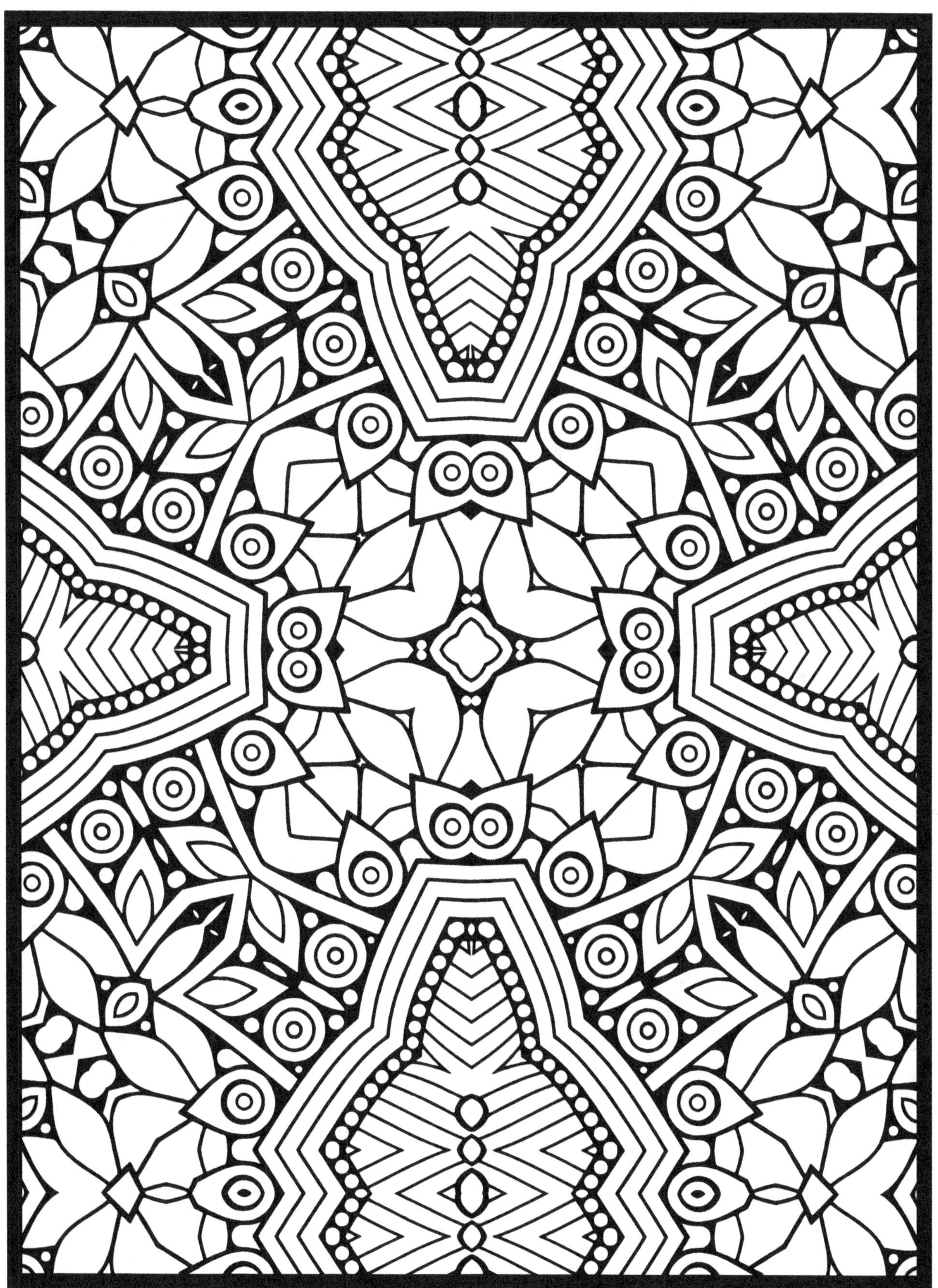

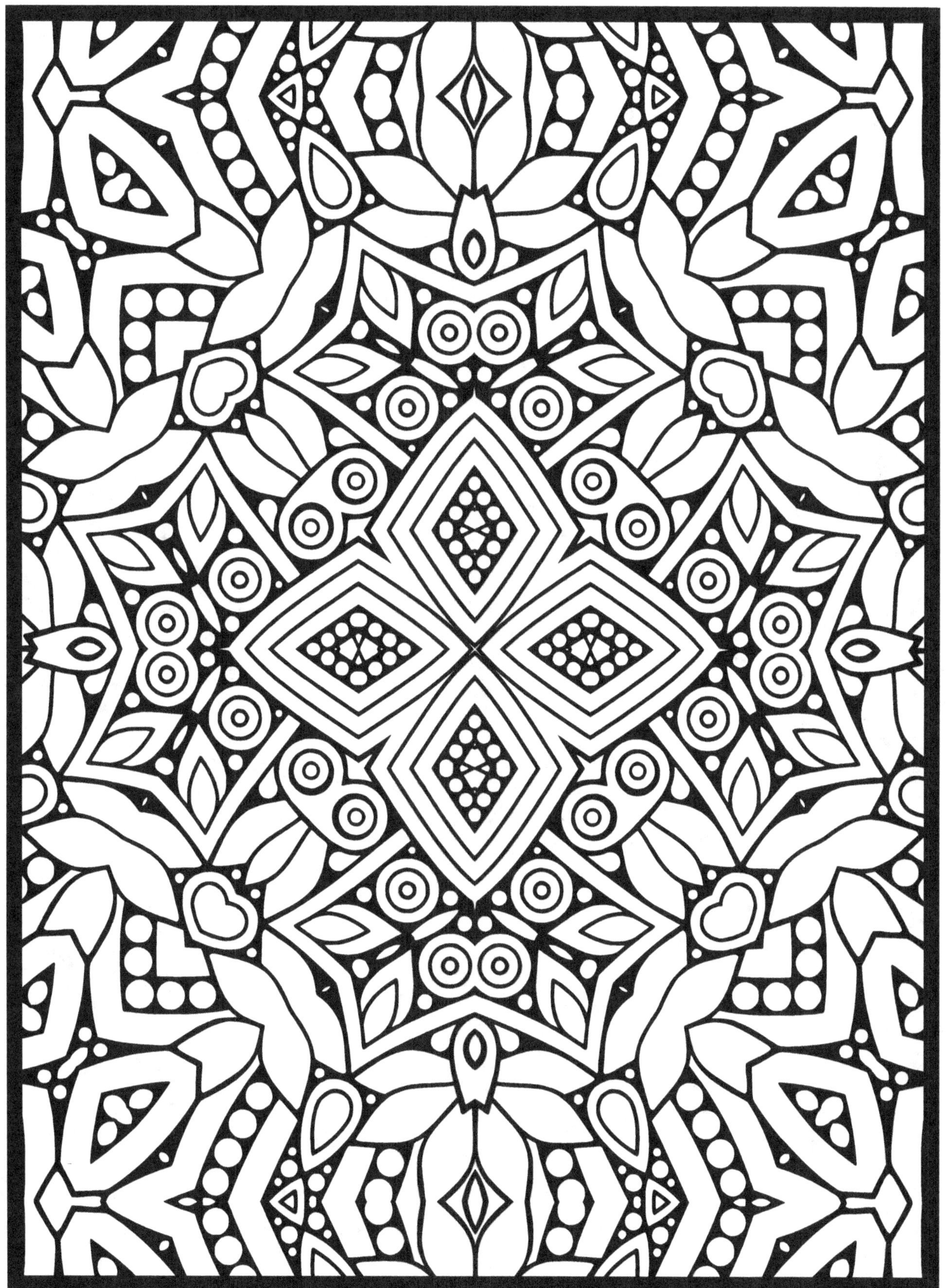

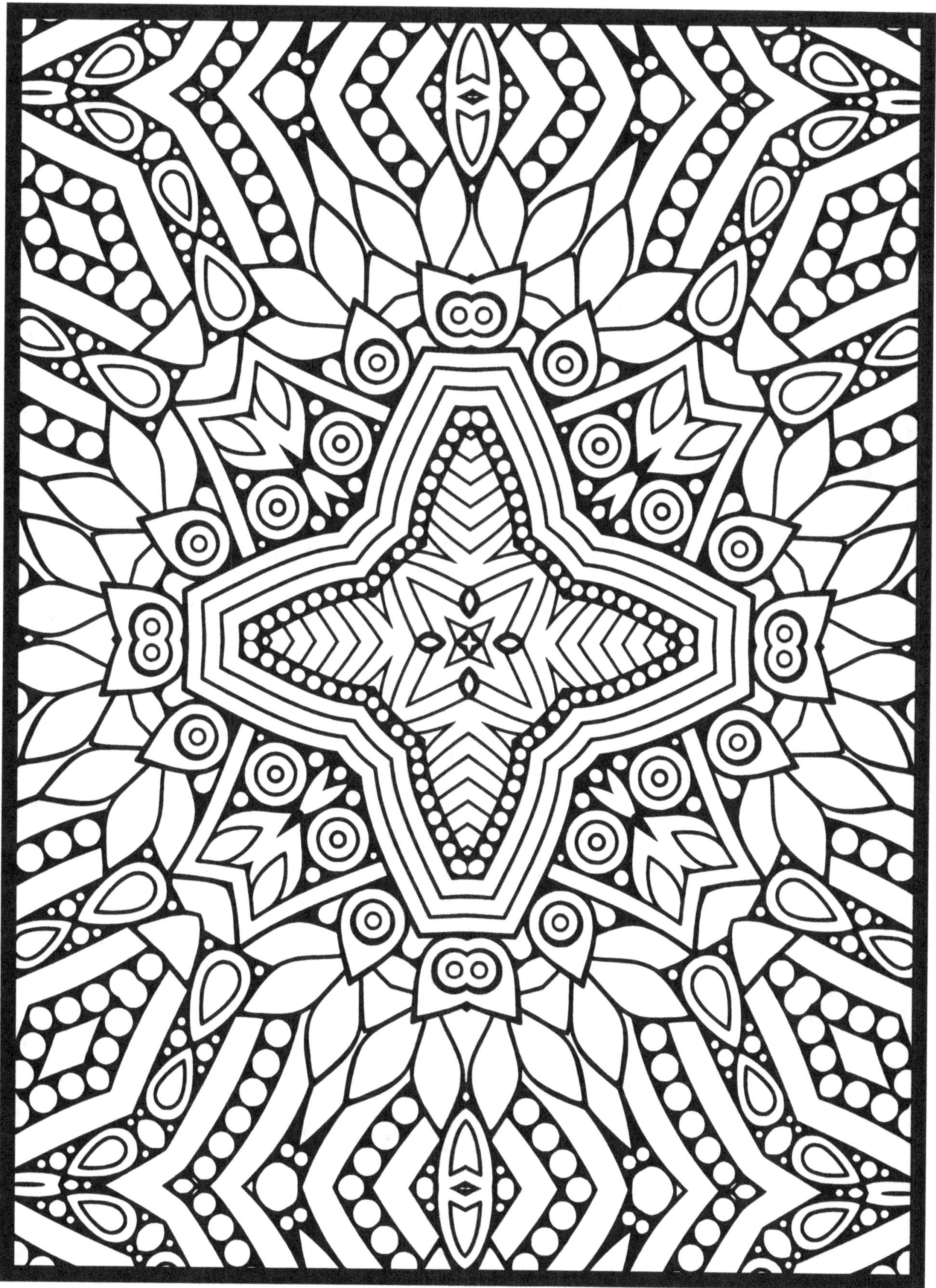

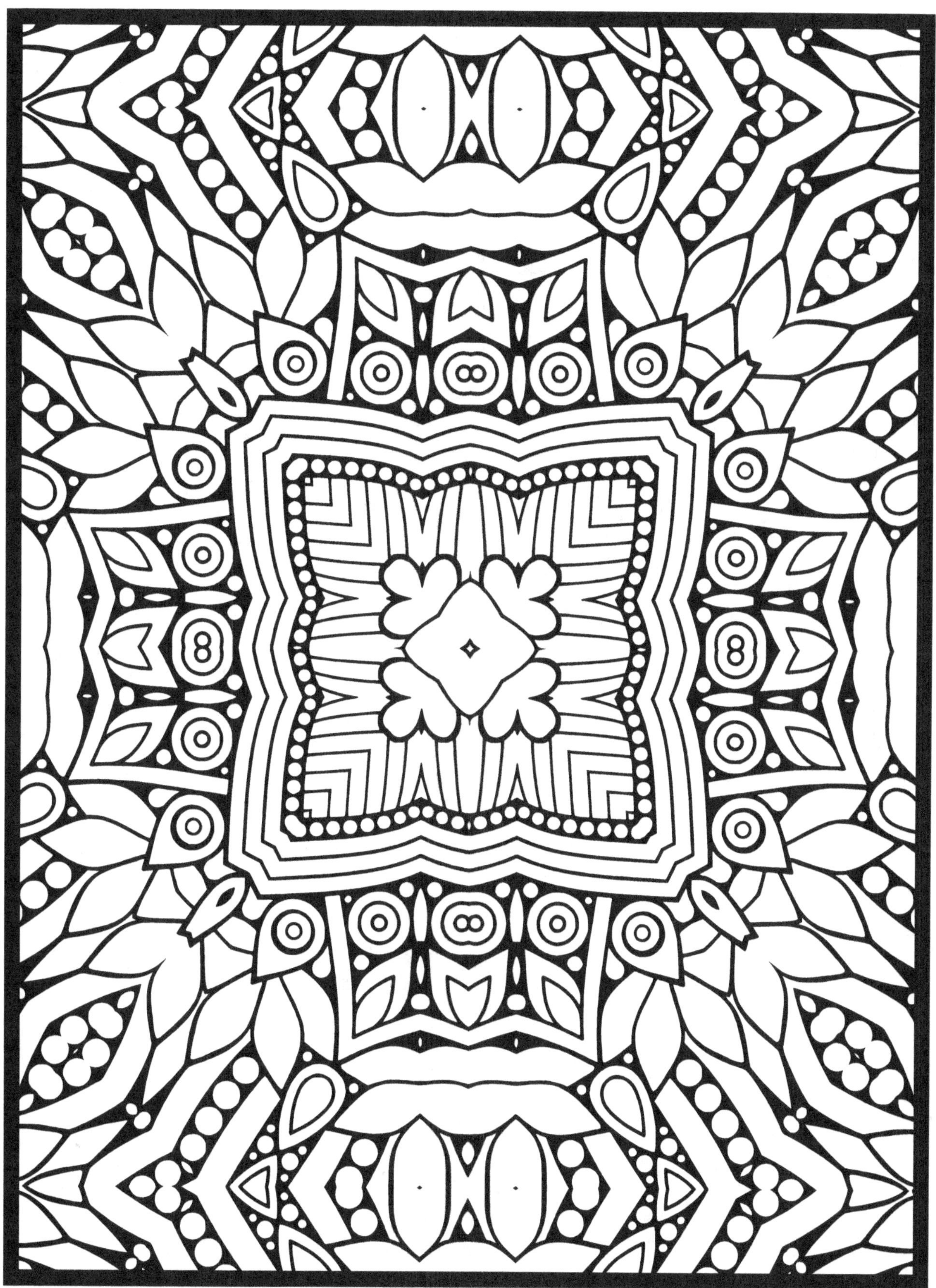

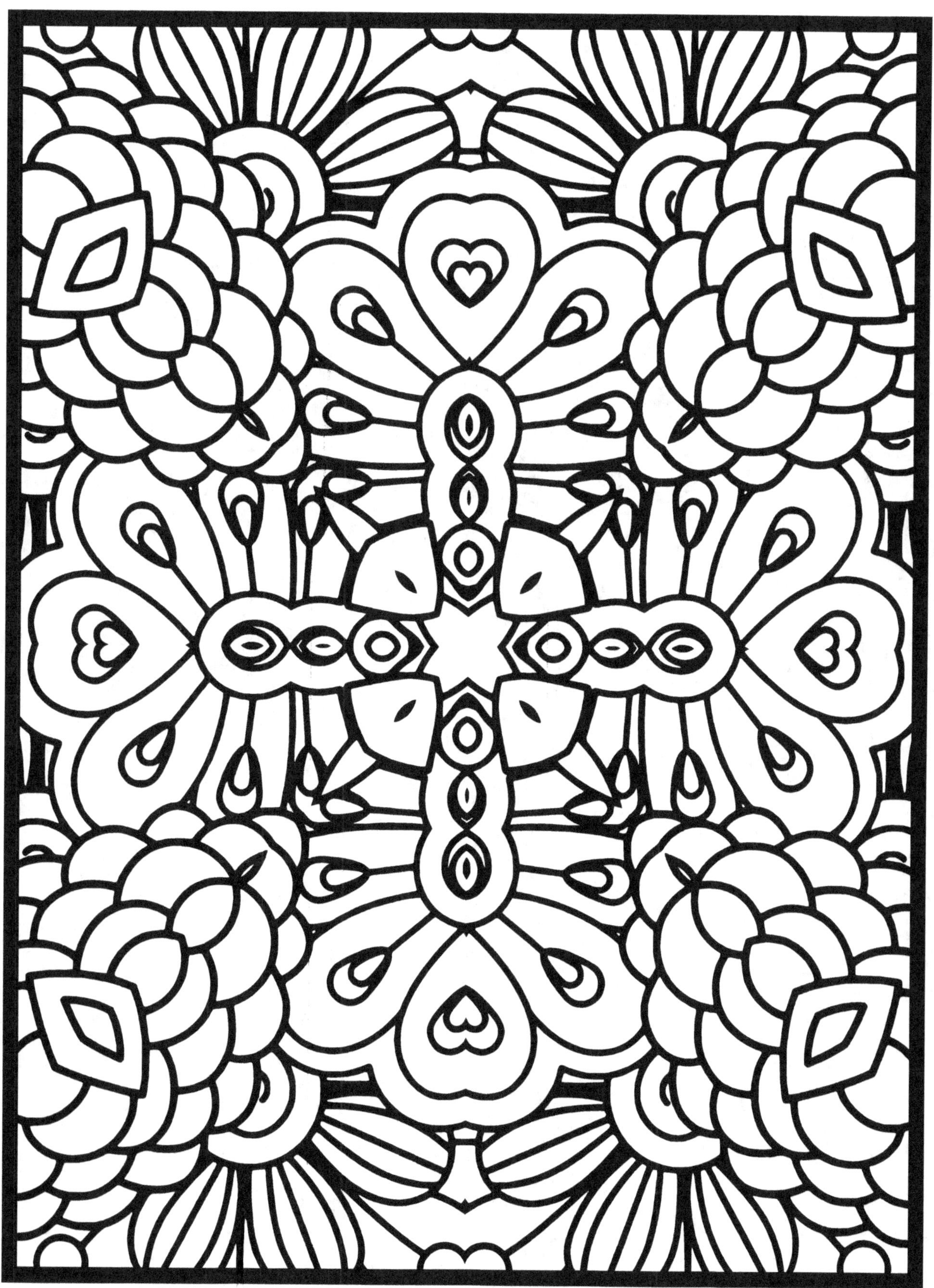

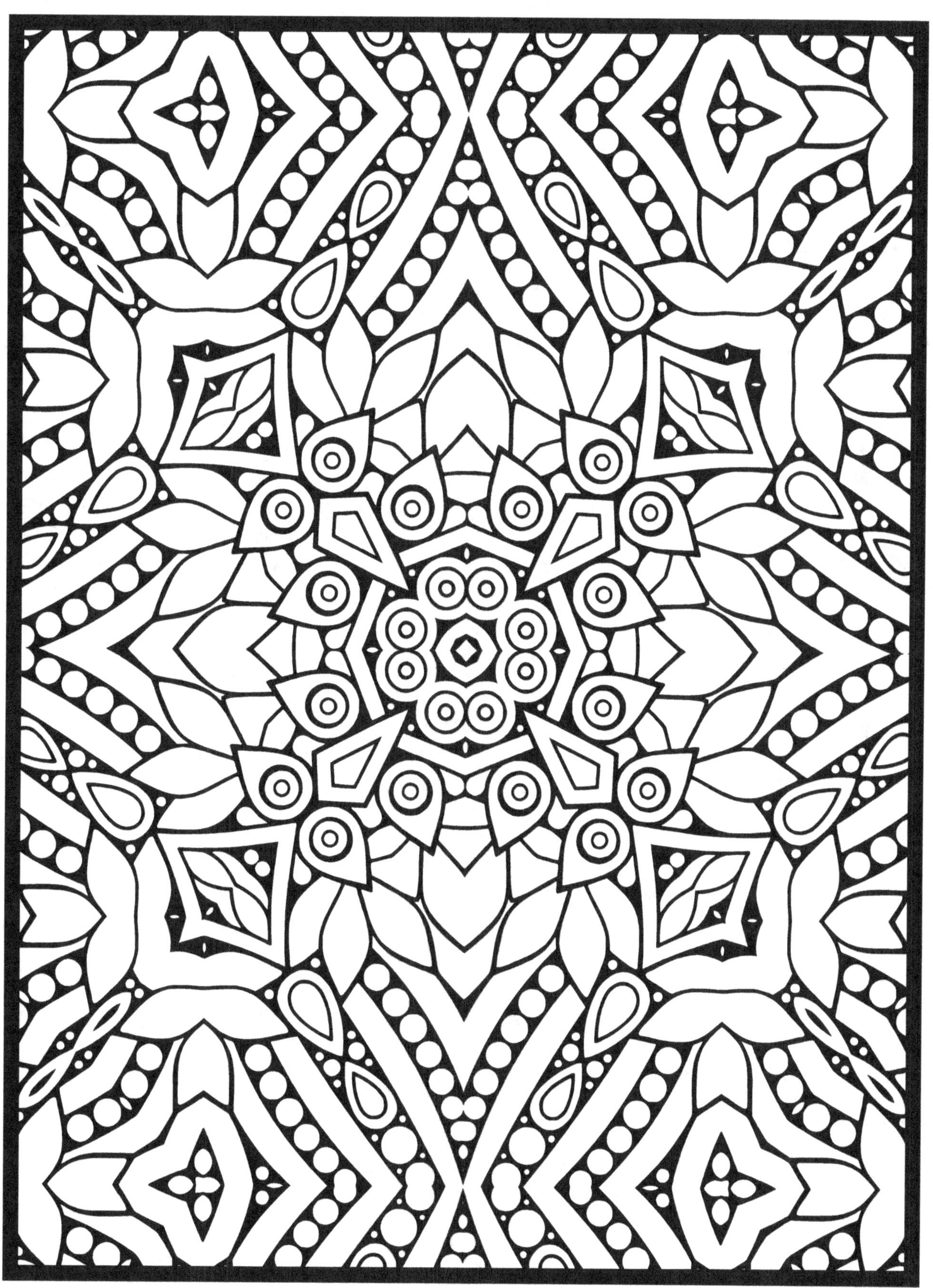

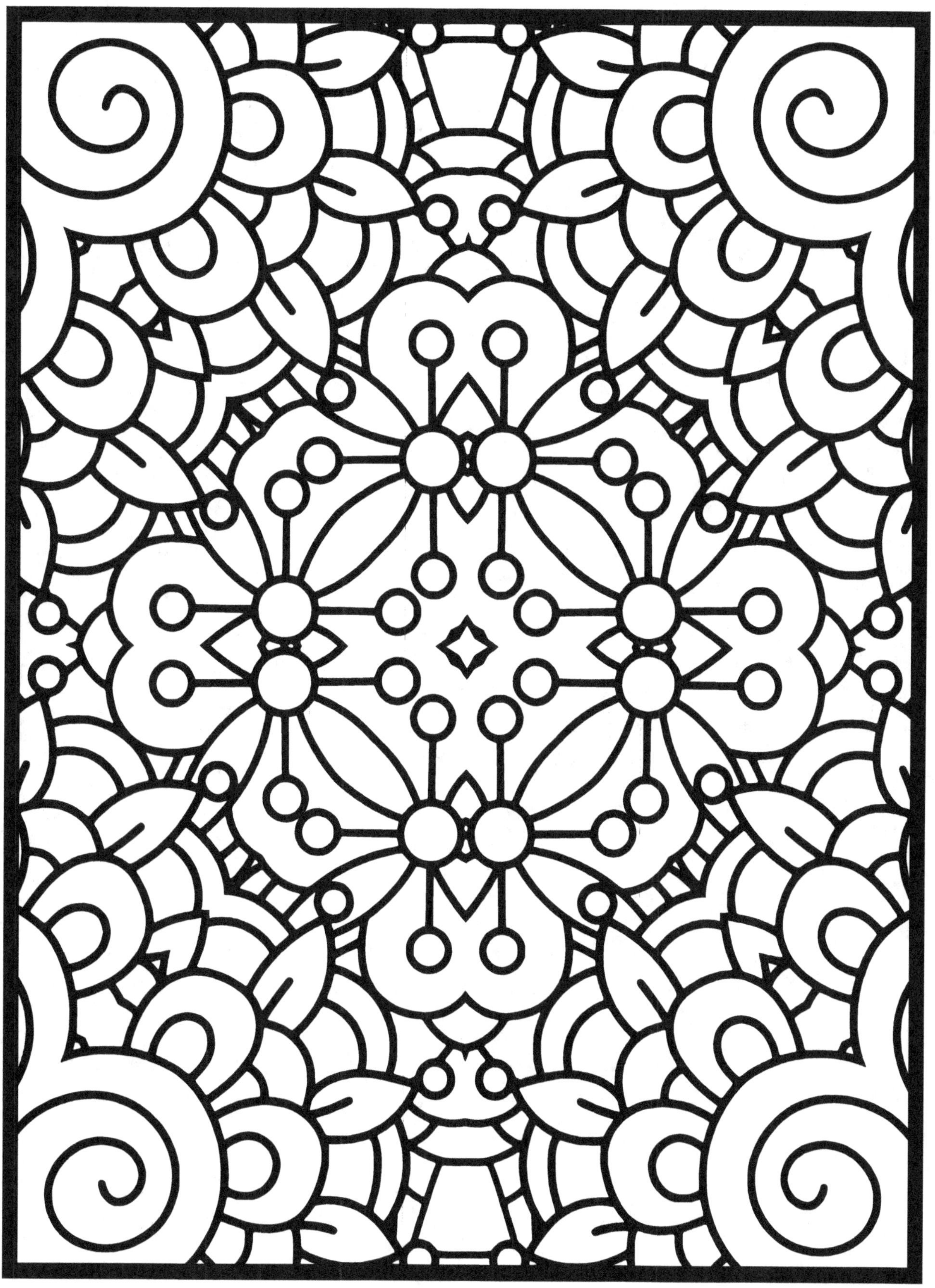

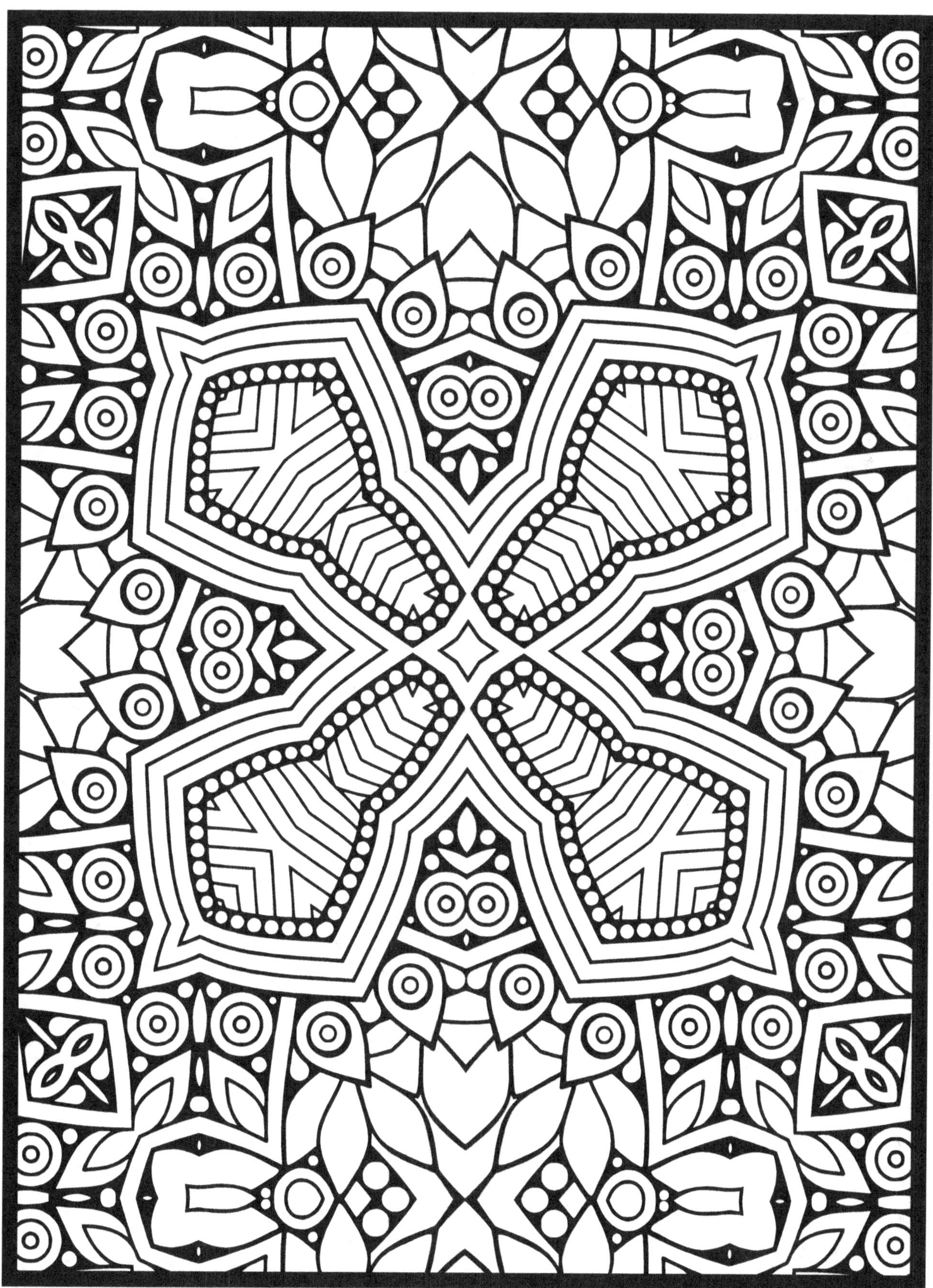

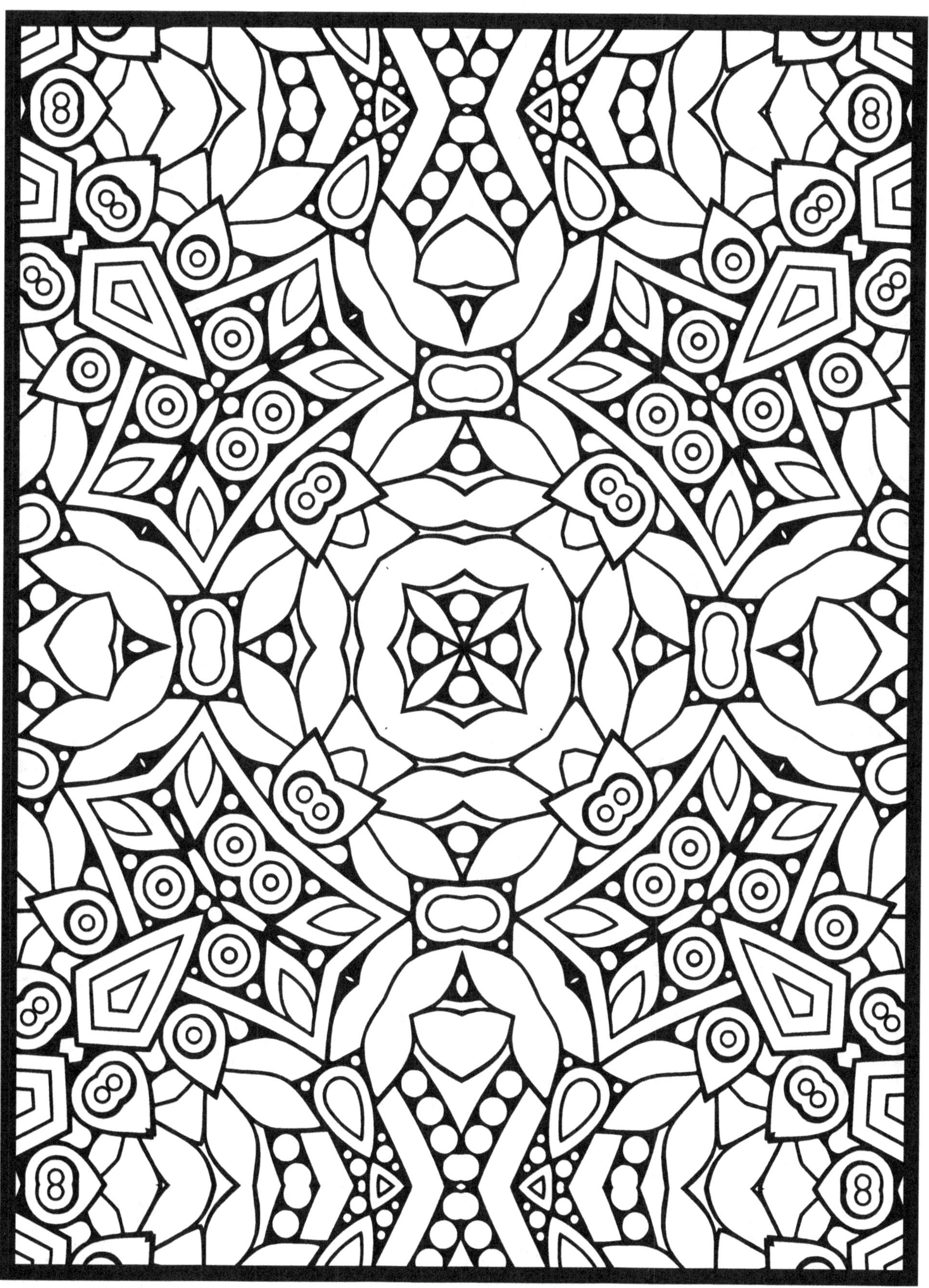

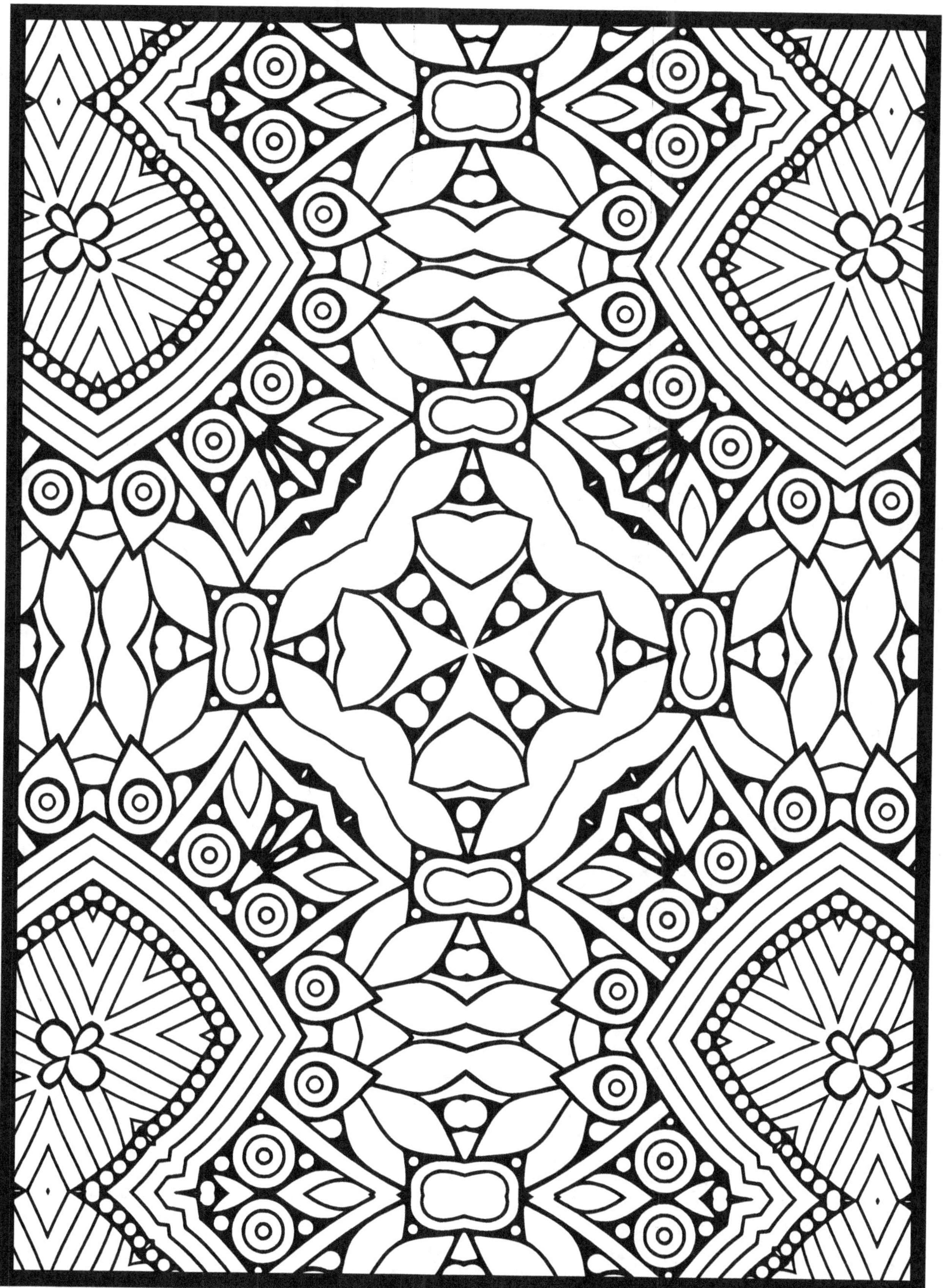

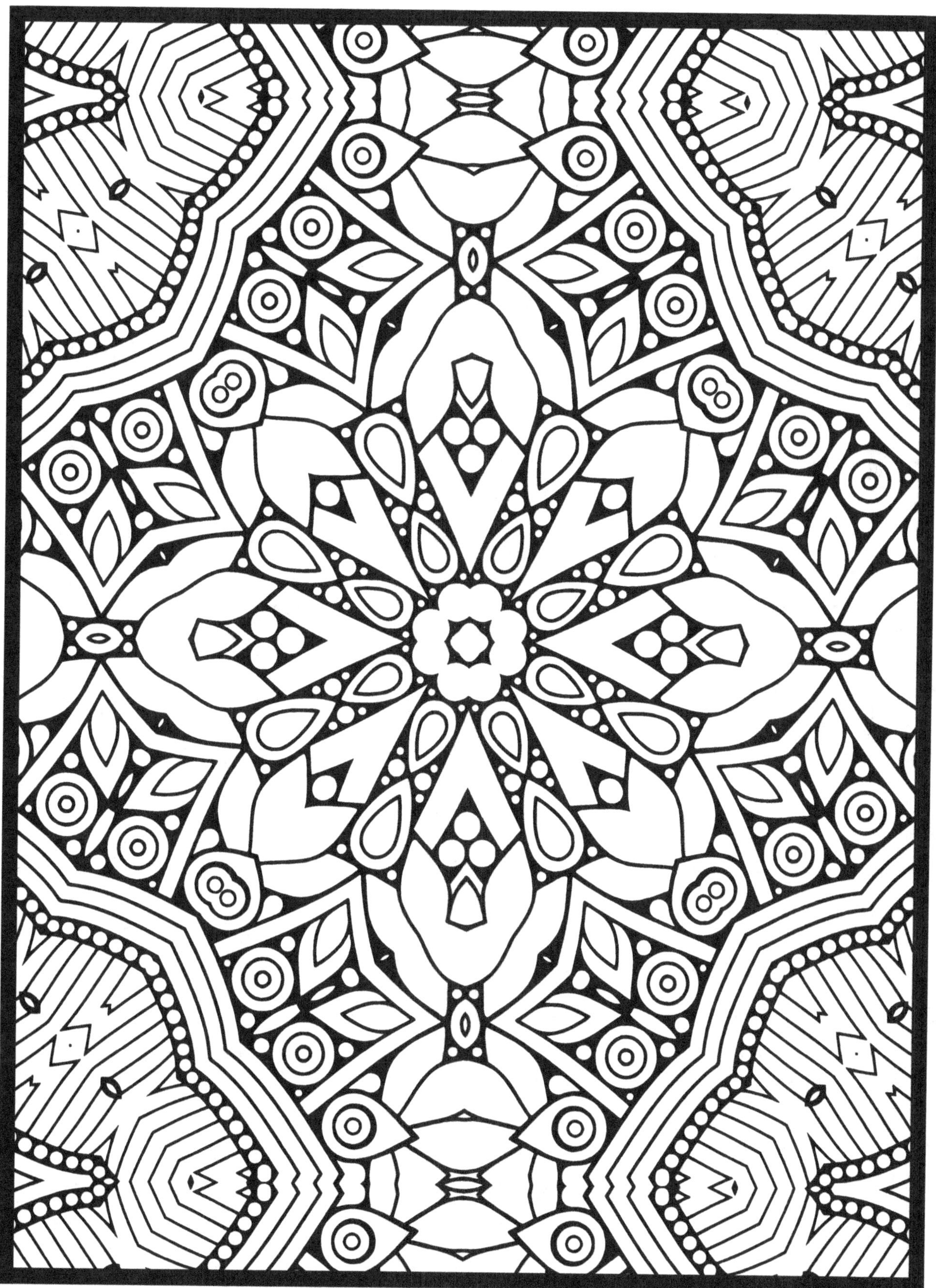

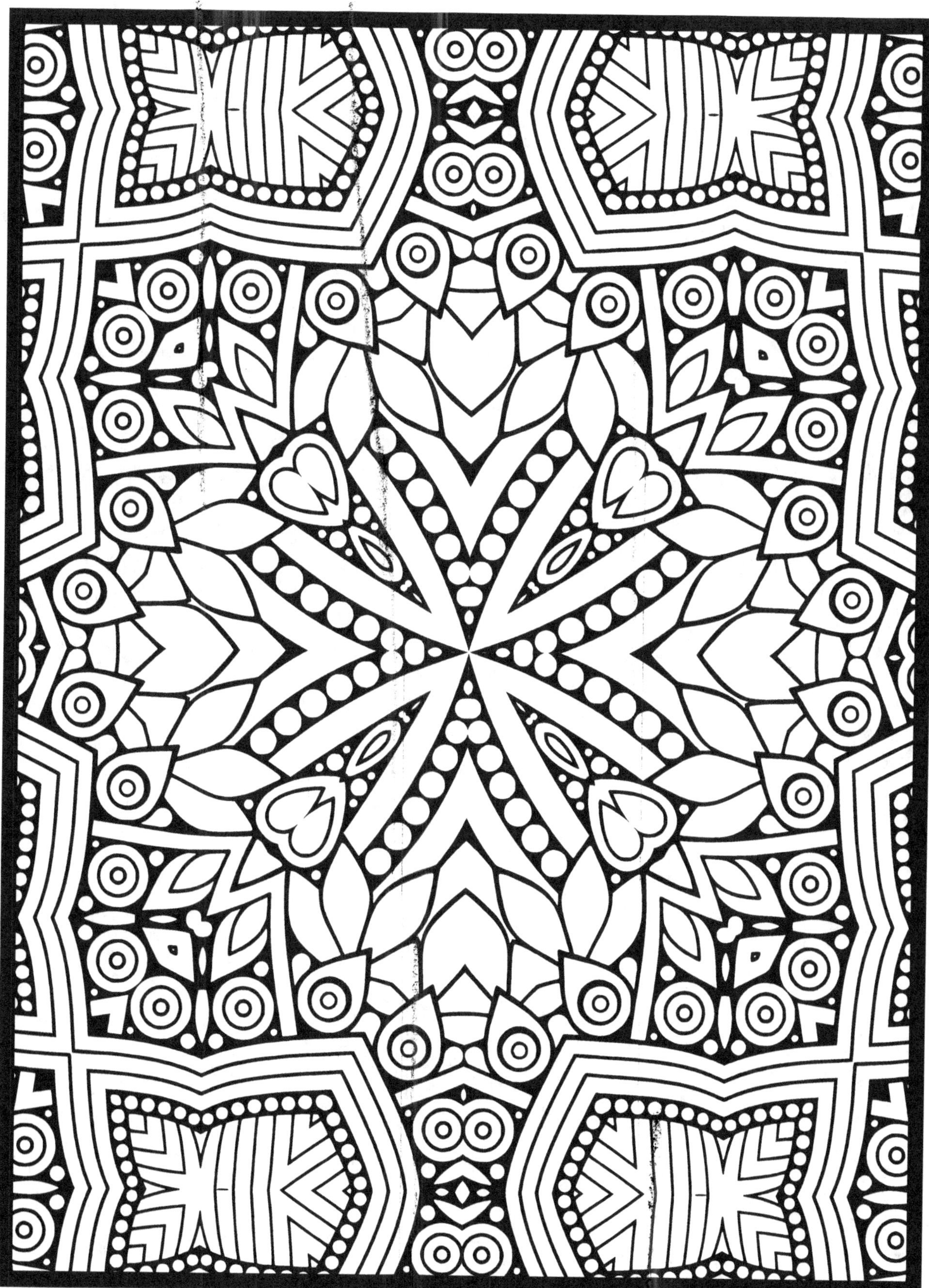

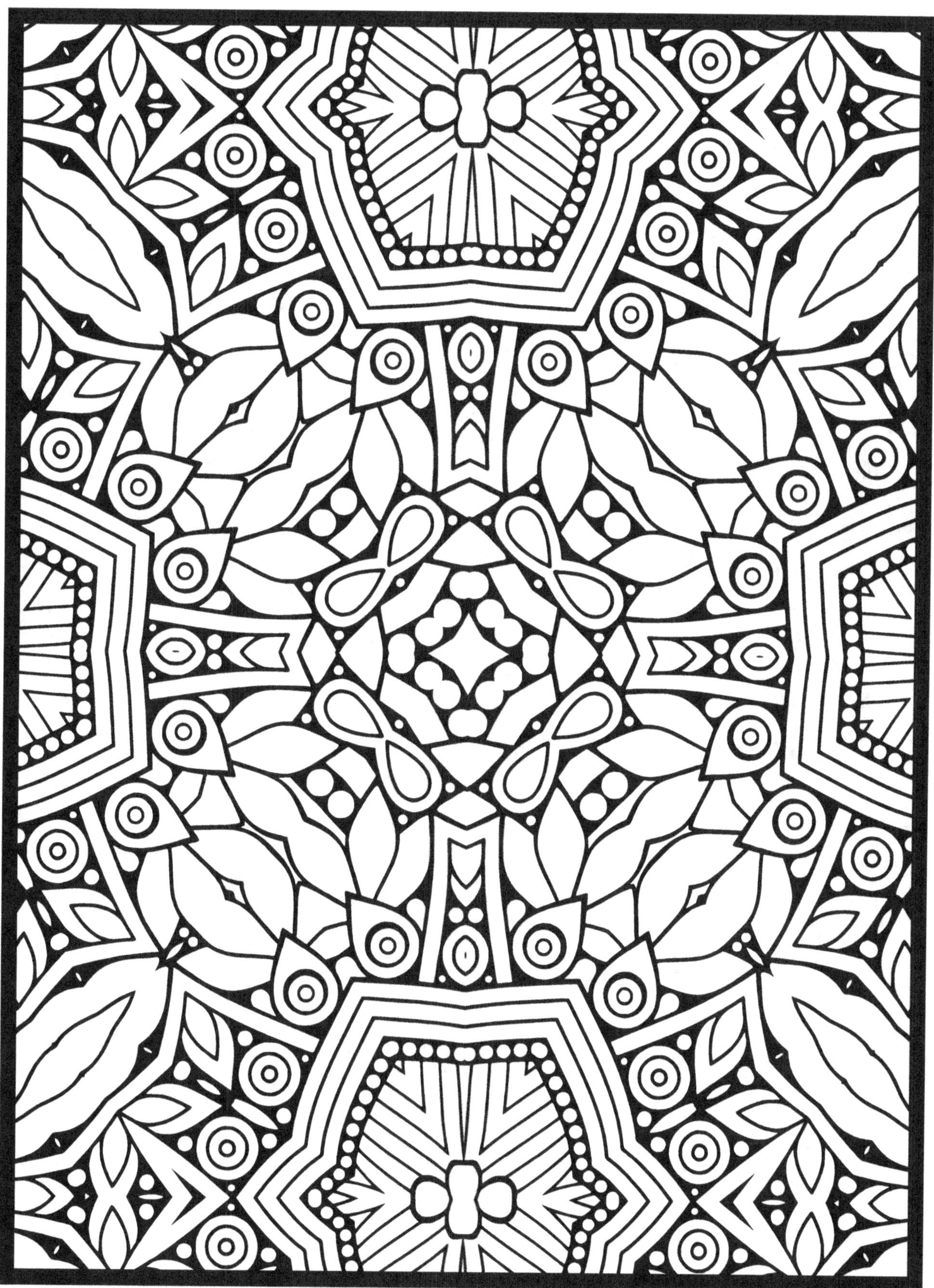

www.ingramcontent.com/pod-product-compliance
Lightning Source LLC
Chambersburg PA
CBHW081623250726
48657CB00009B/2705